DREAMERS WHO DO

DREAMERS
who
DO.

LANNOO
CAMPUS

This book was originally published in Dutch
and French under the title *Dreamers who Do*
(LannooCampus Publishers, 2018).

D/2019/45/89
ISBN 978 94 014 5347 9
NUR 808, 770

Cover and interior design
Annemie Mermans | Meer wit, www.meerwit.be

Translation
Ian Connerty

LannooCampus Publishers is a subsidiary of
Lannoo Publishers, the book and multimedia division
of Lannoo Publishers nv.

LANNOOCAMPUS PUBLISHERS
ERASME RUELENSVEST 179 BOX 101
3001 LEUVEN, BELGIUM
WWW.LANNOOCAMPUS.BE

DEDICATED TO

Justine, Louis, Margot, Camille and Jef
— *the next generation*

'I was part of Hilde's team at Kemira, until both of us were forced to leave in 2008. The years I worked with her sowed the seeds for my further growth, both as a business leader and as a person. The way Hilde shaped the team was light years removed from the standard business culture of the time and – if I may be frank – from the culture in the majority of organizations today. Hilde not only sees the potential in you before you can see it yourself. She also gives you the confidence to make your way in the business world, while still remaining 100% true to your own deepest drivers. For Hilde, personal growth and business growth go hand in hand. She teaches you to follow your own star. I have been telling Hilde for the past ten years that she should write a book about her approach. And now she has finally done it. The model that she develops in the following pages gives concrete form to what she has been doing intuitively all her working life: helping people to unlock their dreams.'

PHILIPPE COGNET, *Sales Director at Italpollina*

CONTENTS

FOREWORD
THE MODEL

This book is the result of a longing, of a deep desire in me. It is rooted in a message I want to share with as many people as I can. People who are close to me, but also people I have never met:

A DREAM LIVES IN EACH OF US.
I BELIEVE THAT EVERYONE POSSESSES AN UNRIVALLED POWER,
AN OFTEN UNKNOWN POTENTIAL TO REALIZE THAT DREAM,
WITH THE HELP OF OTHERS.
WHEN PEOPLE REALIZE THEIR DREAM, CIRCLES OF SAFETY
ARE CREATED THAT INSPIRE OTHERS TO DO THE SAME.
IF MORE PEOPLE ARE ABLE TO REALIZE THEIR DREAMS,
THE WORLD WILL BECOME A BETTER PLACE.

I needed useable tools to inspire people with my belief and prompt them to take action. And so I went in search of a model. But let me first tell you a story or two.

My Lenny Kravitz story

JUST AFTER I GRADUATED, I fell head over heels – not that I was such a hip chick, but it happened anyway – for Lenny Kravitz and his music. The first of his numbers I ever heard was 'Let Love Rule'. I was gripped, blown away. That song expressed so powerfully the drive that had always made me want to stand up for the weakest people around me. The message, packaged in marvellous music that not only suffused my mind but filled my entire body, cemented my resolve: 'Together, we can change the world'. I followed Lenny Kravitz throughout that period. Not just for his lyrics, but above all for his music and for the sheer artistry of his playing. The more I got to know his music, the more I learnt about the man – and the greater my admiration became. His grandfather had taught him that no goal is unachievable if you climb the stairway that leads to its realization a step at a time. Lenny Kravitz writes nearly all his music himself. And he has learnt to play all the instruments in his songs, apart from the wind ones. He is a perfectionist when it comes to the things he creates. For the things he can't do himself, he surrounds himself with experts, the very best in the business: from the horn player to the backing vocals, even the photographer... and everyone else.

When in a later phase of my life I wanted to explore 'what makes people tick', I returned to Lenny's texts. In their deep wisdom I read my own beliefs, the entire message that forms the basis for this book. What an example he set of doing, of acting, of implementing! His words seemed to embody everything you need to know about how to start from an image of the way you would like things to be – your dream – and how you can make it come true through discipline, expertise and perseverance. Together with others. In short, Lenny Kravitz became my soul mate. As he once said in an interview, Let Love Rule is the core of his philosophy of life.

The more I looked at people in an analytical manner, the better I understood that we can all realize our dream in different ways and by different routes. Music, literature, philosophy, art, sculpture, religion: it doesn't really matter. And that brings me to my second story.

My Koen Vanmechelen story

MY MOTHER HAS ALWAYS LOVED ART. Already as a young woman, she knew her Rodin and Zadkine. She hung around in Middelheim Park. She went to exhibitions in Antwerp. One year, she even followed evening classes at the art academy. Convinced that our true passions in life only become evident as we get older, she made sure that her children were likewise exposed to as much art as possible.

As the daughter of a chicken farmer, she also had a close affinity with chickens. Perhaps this explains why when the conceptual artist Koen Vanmechelen launched his 'Cosmopolitan Chicken Project' in the early years of the new century, a number of other pieces in my life's puzzle fell into place. The 'Cosmopolitan Chicken Project' (CCP) is a metaphorical project rooted in cultural and genetic diversity. The idea of creating a new cosmopolitan or hybrid chicken by cross-breeding all the different types of chicken in the world simply blew my mind. It still does. Started in 1999, the most recent crossbreed – the Mechelse Maatiaiskana – contains the genes of no fewer than 21 other breeds. And the end is by no means in sight.

Apart from the CCP, I was also deeply moved at that time by the story of the Cosmogolem. This four-metre tall wooden giant represents a figure from Jewish legend, who did what he could to help mankind. The enthusiasm with which I once heard Koen Vanmechelen talk about this project had a huge impact on me. The Cosmogolem – which has been erected at more than 30 locations worldwide – is a symbol of empowerment. Its aim is to make people – and particularly children – who live in unfortunate circumstances stronger. They can share their wishes and dreams with the giant, in whatever manner they wish. Some do it with a song or a dance. Others do it with a poem or a drawing...

Like Lenny Kravitz, Koen Vanmechelen has become a fellow traveller of mine. I have been to all his exhibitions in Belgium, our common homeland. I have read everything I can find about him. Not only about the artist, but also about the man and how he grew as a person through his art. I was impressed by the ambition of his 'Cosmopolitan Chicken Project' and the way in which he involved experts from dozens of different domains. When I began to see an overlap between the Cosmogolem symbolism and what I was also starting to tell people about leadership and self-leadership, for me the wheel had come full circle.

In the meantime, Koen Vanmechelen has been working tirelessly for decades to help people who are burdened by a difficult past to find a voice and a language of their own. For example, through his partnership with The Future of Hope, he participates actively in the dreams of people who want to exchange their role as victim for greater responsibility for their own future and for the future of others who have had the same false start in life as themselves. Together with founder Chido Govera (who also experienced a troubled past as an orphan), he dreams of creating a Future of Hope network, first across Africa and later across the entire world. The aim is to provide as many people as possible with an income and to eradicate hunger from the world by making better use of the resources that are available locally. The mother house in Harare (Zimbabwe) is a training centre where orphans learn how to grow edible mushrooms. But they are also taught crucial life skills, like social behaviour, dealing with sexuality, AIDS and hygiene.

What a wonderful way to give shape and form to your dream of changing the world! And what a marvellous effort to try and make that world a better place! Koen Vanmechelen: 'Art is never obligation-free. It opens your mind and broadens your perspective. It can free people from their chains. Art creates responsibility.' Koen Vanmechelen the man and Koen Vanmechelen the artist: two 'Dreamers who Do'.

Music, the visual arts, theatre: they all speak to different parts of the brain than a discourse in words. Art appeals directly to our subconscious. It moves first our hearts and only then our minds. First our intuition and then the brain. During the early first phase of *Dreamers who Do* a strong appeal was sent out by the songs of Lenny Kravitz and the projects of Koen Vanmechelen.

In particular, four songs by Lenny Kravitz grew almost organically to become the backbone for my model: **DREAM, STAND, PUSH, LET LOVE RULE.** The vision I developed on this basis is very simple:

TO REALIZE YOUR DREAM, THIS IS WHAT YOU MUST DO:
TAKE THREE STEPS: DREAM, STAND, PUSH.
KEEP ONE THING CLEARLY IN SIGHT: LET LOVE RULE.
THIS WILL LEAD YOU FROM YOUR AMBITION TO YOUR GOAL.

In the following four chapters I will take you on a journey. During this journey, we will tap into, strengthen and make active the dream-fulfilling potential that is in all of us. Koen Vanmechelen will offer his reflections on the different stages of our travels. In each chapter he will provide us with a work of art and a statement that serve as an oasis of rest and tranquility in my story.

Music finds its own way to the heart. Images speak for themselves. I need words. But the message is the same. And together we will reach more people every day.

DREAM,

All men dream: but not equally. Those who dream by night in the dusty recesses of their minds wake in the day to find that it was vanity: but the dreamers of the day are dangerous men, for they may act upon their dreams with open eyes, to make it possible.

T.E. LAWRENCE *(1888-1935), prose writer, archaeologist and soldier – better known as 'Lawrence of Arabia'*

GO IN SEARCH OF THE DREAM THAT LIVES WITHIN YOU

THERE IS JUST ONE CONDITION THAT NEEDS TO BE FULFILLED BEFORE YOU CAN REALIZE YOUR DREAM. YOU MUST FIRST BE ABLE TO SEE IT!

We humans are visual animals. Simple neurological processes determine that our brains only begin to work if we can imagine ourselves in some other or some new situation. In that order. It is the seeing of something other or something new that prompts us into action. If we are not able to see it, nothing happens.

There was once a time when you went in search of your dreams free from all inhibitions; in which you constantly went looking for the biotope in which you were one with the deepest core of your being; in which, in other words, you were in direct touch with the things that made you happiest. This golden time was your childhood. Almost instinctively, you moved towards the things that made you complete and you made plans for later. Did you grow up in an environment that offered you support and stimulation? If so, you grew in fertile ground and perhaps you are already busy integrating your dream into your adult life. Perhaps, however, your life story has been more difficult, bedevilled by limitations, obstacles and disruptive factors that have distracted you and pushed you off course. In that case, you will need to travel a greater distance to achieve the fragile dream of your early years. But in the end, it doesn't really matter. It makes no difference whether your journey is short or long. At the end of the road, you will still reap the same reward: you will see that the tender shoots of your dream are still alive inside you today.

If I ask **my mother** what she used to dream about as a child, she says she has no idea. "In our family of eight children – I had two brothers and five sisters – only two things were really important: being well-behaved and getting on with each other. If we respected those rules, for the rest of the time we could pretty much do what we liked. We had a lot of freedom and I had no real need or desire to live inside my head. I didn't have a real dream about what I wanted to be when I grew up or how I would live my life. As time passed, an urge gradually developed inside of me and I knew that I wanted to look after children. But a man didn't really feature in that plan. Who knows? If I hadn't met Staf, maybe I would have become a single mother!"

By the time she finished secondary school, my mother wanted to become a nurse, but you had to be eighteen to register for the training and she was too young (she had skipped a year at school). And so she decided to train as a nursery teacher instead. She wasn't even twenty by the time she had finished her studies. Her entire career was devoted to fighting for the rights of children: in other words, making sure that children had everything she believed they needed to be happy. You could say that she found the way to fulfilment in her life intuitively, whereas more recent generations often need to search more explicitly for that fulfilment. Later, when she looked back on those years, she concluded that if she had a dream at all, it would be to care for neglected children. Or perhaps run an orphanage. But she never really stopped to think about it. My mother is a woman of action. Her motto is 'carry on regardless' and that is what she has always done. Her day is a non-stop succession of actions, with only an occasional pause for 'a little dream', something to look forward to.

DID I HAVE A DREAM AS A CHILD? I think that I already knew in my second to last year of primary school: I wanted to be a mother. I must have been about thirteen before a second image lodged itself in my mind. I no longer wanted to be 'just' a mother; I wanted to be a paediatrician. I could see it all in my mind: I would build a house from which I could run my practice, with a glass partition wall that would allow me to see my children and their nanny while I was working. The glass wall idea gave me the feeling that I could manage everything all at the same time. I have always wanted to care for everyone and everything around me. Friends, the kids next door, classmates: I was ready to help and defend them all! I had a very open, almost boundless view of the world: I was brought up in a home where everyone was welcome and where there was always room for one more under my mother's protective wing. I thought that this was the way life worked and had no idea that it could be anything different.

From my teenage years onward, I systematically went in search of complex things. Simplifying those things gave me a kick. I always set the bar high for myself – as high as possible. When the time came to decide what I wanted to study at university, I was torn between civil engineering – to my mind, the most difficult discipline of all – and medicine. The pendulum very quickly swung in favour of the former. The entrance examination coincided with our six-form school trip to Rome, but I did the exam anyway: Rome could wait. I managed to scrape a pass – but only just. There were no more than a handful of girls in our intake and all the boys were really bright sparks. But I had no time to worry about that. The academic year was about to start. I wanted to show the world that everything is possible, as long as you want it badly enough.

Lenny Kravitz's song 'Dream' may have been inspired by religion – like the singer himself – but from start to finish it reflects the power and the persistence of the dream that lives inside each and every one of us, slowly taking shape before finally finding its own way out into the big, wide world.

LENNY KRAVITZ. Dream

You can take away my freedom
But my spirit will run free
You can take away my vision
That don't mean that I can't see

Well all I have to say
Is it doesn't work that way
What lives inside of me
Will find its way to be

It all starts with a dream
The dawn of a new day
The God inside of you
Will always see you through
So hold on to your dream
No one can take the dream
From your heart
From your heart

You can try to shake my reason
But you'll never take me down
You can fill me full of bullets
But I'm built on solid ground

So all I have to say
Is I'm not going away
It's much bigger than me
God's will will always be

Amen, amen, amen

You will never take my passion
'Cause it always will remain
Even if I lose this battle, oh yeah
It's just blood inside my veins

That's all I have to say
The dream won't go away
You can't steal from me
What God gave me for free

The instinctive urge and the myriad small dreams of my mother, my own early dreams – they would later turn out to be purely symbolic: my sister's children might call me their 'extra-mum', but that is the closest I have ever got to motherhood – and the gift from God's hand that lives in your heart, as Lenny Kravitz puts it: these are just a few of the many forms that a dream can take. They are just so many names for those little pieces of yourself, which, once you begin to tap into them, will release a potential that can take you to heights you never imagined possible. We sometimes talk about a passion, a purpose, a voice that emerges through your talent, perhaps even 'your own language'. As Koen Vanmechelen says: 'It is only when we discover our own language that we are able to acquire knowledge and break out of our cage. If you fail to do this, you will end up building walls around your own thoughts and use all your energy against yourself. When that happens, the only answer is a scream.'

1.
YOUR DREAM IS CLEAR — THE WAY TO ITS REALIZATION IS OPEN

Some people instinctively follow their hearts. What they do perfectly matches what they feel. They are reliable, authentic and in balance with themselves. In short, the kind of men and women you want to follow. Almost unconsciously, they attract other people to them, spurring those others to act and inspiring them to live out their dream. If you ask them, they are able to visualize what they see themselves doing in the years ahead. Each day, they work at what in my model I call 'the painting of their life'. Everything they do revolves around a single core purpose: their mission in life, their WHY. You can clearly see their talent in all their actions. Their inner compass directs their norms and values, their identity, working as a filter that decides what will be allowed to pass and what not.

I can think of no finer example than the 'compass made flesh' that is Charles-Antoine Janssen. Although he never talks about it, it is well known that this scion of the Janssen family – which since the creation of the Belgian state has been active in the banking world and subsequently formed an alliance through marriage with the powerful Solvay family – is charged with the administration of a huge fortune. But this does not prevent him from seeking to achieve self-fulfilment by striving each and every day to pursue his own deepest passions, making full use of his intellectual and spiritual development and his skills in the fields of management, finance and business. When I asked him how he would personally fill in the first of the four steps of the *Dreamers who Do* model, this is what happened:

***Charles-Antoine** asks if it is possible to first take a few moments to concentrate on what he wants to tell me. When I say that this is fine, he sets the alarm on his cell phone for ten minutes, moves his chair slightly away from the table that separates us, places both hands on his knees in a position of symmetrical repose, and closes his eyes. During the next ten minutes, he seems to be going through various states of mind: one moment he seems to be in a kind of restless sleep; the next moment, he nods gently and raises his head to a more erect position, accompanied by a trance-like swallowing. Different cycles of concentration and meditation appear to be alternating in his head, until the moment when the alarm sounds, bringing to an end these different stages of consciousness. Without looking at me, he takes a pen and a piece of paper and starts writing furiously. The page soon becomes a confused battleground of words, circles, arrows and connections, some of which, following further thought, are later scrapped. I am witnessing a mental journey that involves both doggedness and patient determination, which after a further ten minutes results in a schematic summary of what DREAM means for him. He finally restores the contact between us that was broken some twenty minutes ago, looks at me with deep intensity and – almost as if he is projecting a carefully designed stream of consciousness in my direction – starts his discourse.*

'My grandmother was chair of the Red Cross in Belgium. She was a loving, socially engaged and remarkably disciplined and rigorous woman. It was she who first awoke the seeds of social awareness in me. Her influence was continued by my mother, who took me along as a young child when she made her food distribution visits with Les Repas sur Roues. I was just 7, 8, 9 years old, but I was witness several times a week to different forms of loneliness, pain, poverty and sadness, images that were destined to arouse in me for the rest of my life a desire to do whatever I could to help the most underprivileged social groups, wherever in the world they might be found. When I was at secondary school, I 'gave up' a few of my lunchtimes to help out at a centre for handicapped people further down the same street. When I was a student at university, I spent half of my holidays working to take care of the homeless and during term time spent some of the hours between my own lessons helping deprived children do their homework

After completing my studies in law and management at Brussels and Harvard, I followed an internship at the Commissariat-General for Refugees and Stateless Persons and worked for a time with Mother Theresa. The way in which she inspired me to 'do small things with great love' further kindled my dream to bring greater humanity and more humanitarianism into our world, a dream that continued to give joy and meaning in my life, time after time.

After a number of years working in companies in Belgium, Germany and the United Kingdom, where I was able to satisfy my youthful ambition to prove that I could stand on my own two feet financially, a journey to Nepal with my brother eventually brought me into contact with Mathieu Ricard and the Dalai Lama. During that unforgettable visit, I met people with a greater clarity of mind and a more boundless aspiration to generate greater humanity – a more integrated form of fellow feeling for each other – than I had ever met before. It was as though the daily exercise of contemplation and meditation had programmed these people to think differently. My experiences then strengthened my dream with a new desire for greater contact with the earth, myself and the light. I now wanted to link my personal wish to be in harmony with my own deepest passions to the benefits of strong management skills.

With the aim of assisting innovative social projects – the concept of 'donating expertise' that was already well known in Anglo-Saxon countries particularly appealed to me – in 2003 I founded ToolBox with three of my good friends. In the meantime, ToolBox has been providing a framework, methodology and the necessary tools for the efficient support of organizations active in the Belgian social sector for more than 14 years. ToolBox works with 150 professionals who are willing to make their expertise available to these organizations on a voluntary basis. In 2010, I also founded Kois Invest with another friend, which effectively laid the first stone for the foundations of a fundamentally new form of social finance, known as impact investment.

Our activities are based on three central pillars: the offering of advice, the structuring of innovative social projects in the financial field and the management of Dedicated Funds. In both these companies I can see aspects of the dream that has been my mainstay since childhood.

In 2007, Charles-Antoine Janssen was also responsible for setting up ToolBox India and in 2016 he moved to that country with his family to open an Asian office of Kois Invest, with ambitious plans to remedy huge social needs, particularly in the field of health care, which have arisen because of the inefficiency of the Indian government. In 2013, I was asked to take on the chair of ToolBox Belgium. I have never been so proud in all my life and in the meantime have since begun my second term of office.

People who are able to live their dream are not new to me. I know of several very tangible examples, some of them quite close to home. I can remember, for example, how when we were children my brother Geert used to tell me as we lay awake in bed about his dream of one day building up and running an international breeding centre for horses. Over the years, he has become my prototype for the 'Dreamer who does'.

Geert: *For as long as I can remember, I have had a passion for horses. I was just two when one Sunday in church I began to shout: 'Horse! Horse!' That must have been the start of it, I suppose. I had seen an image of St. Martin on his trusty steed! Since that first time, my fascination with horses has never left me. There used to be two ponies in our street and I went to stand near them whenever I could. And on the road to our grandparent's place in Kruibeke I could point out all the fields where they had horses. One day, I decided that things needed to be made a little more concrete and so I told my parents that I wanted a horse of my own. 'You can have a horse when you are twelve,' said my father, secretly hoping that by then I might have forgotten all about it. But I didn't, of course. When I was twelve, I repeated my request and this time there was no way out for my parents: a promise is a promise. We didn't have room for a horse at home, so we hired a meadow and a stable. One horse* *later became two. I was probably around fourteen when I bought and traded my first horse. Dad put up the money and became the guarantor, but I was allowed to keep the profit. The commercial side of things – doing business, buying and selling – was simply in my blood. When I was still just a lad, I was able to sell a puppy that had been born in our house at the market in Aarschot. And together with Uncle Sooi, who had a dairy farm, I sold dozens and dozens of sheep in the market at Heist-op-den-Berg.*

By the time I was in my twenties, in the village where we lived I had developed a network of contacts of people and friends who had fields and stables for my horses. After work, I travelled around to visit and ride each one of them, occasionally buying or selling a new one when the opportunity arose. A bit later on, I bought a house with its own grounds. I gradually added meadows and built stables and recently we even opened an artificial insemination unit!

Perhaps it was once my dream to make horse breeding and trading my main professional activity, but in recent decades I have never had the urge – not even once – to give up my fulltime job so that I can concentrate on horses. Now that I stop to think about it, in every company where I have ever worked I always enjoyed myself so much that I never felt for a single moment that I 'have to go to work'. It was never a chore or an obligation; it was more like playing, day after day. And it's the same with horses. At one time, I dreamed of becoming a vet. It never happened, but ten years ago my passion moved into my life anyway – in the shape of a lady vet!'

This year for the third time Geert organized a large – and now renowned – international horse auction: the Horseman Elite Auction.

Dreaming in my model is like creating the painting of your life. If you are working towards your dream, you are working on your painting. You see an image and you paint it. You visualize something – something you do, somewhere you go, something around you, something you feel – and so you depict it in your painting. The image is not always the same. In fact, you will be confronted with many different images. Some images will change, grow and evolve. Sometimes a newer image will replace an older one. Because this is the painting of your life, you shouldn't only depict what is, but also what might be and what you would like to be. You are the artist. You are holding the brush. It is your hand that adds to the canvas all the many things that are stirring deep down inside you. And as you become more yourself with each passing day, so you will discover more ideas and more inspiration for your painting. Some things you will add; others you will take away. Your painting is never finished.

WHEN I WAS TEN, I PAINTED MYSELF IN MY MIND'S EYE AS A MOTHER. A few years later, I added a second element to my painting, when I saw my future home with the glass wall that allowed my future doctor self to keep an eye on my children while I was working.

As time passed, more and more images were added to other parts of my canvas. To be honest, I think that I have never really stopped working on it and I am certain that this makes me a fortunate person. People who find themselves in difficult situations with no prospect of a better life do not have the time, the material or the mental inclination to paint. This is the reason why people in poverty sometimes prefer to spend their meagre resources on one or two luxury items, so that for just a few brief moments they can once again feel that they are in control of what they want to do. As long as they are unable to visualize themselves in a better situation, their painting will remain unfinished: without visualization there can be no hope and without hope there is no strength to carry on with the work of change. People who live in unfortunate circumstances are therefore those who need the support of others more than anyone else. 'Let love rule'.

Visualizing your dream is the first step towards its realization.

What a wonderful sound to wake up to. The woodcutter is underneath my window, setting about the felled tree with his axe. It is like waking up back in the good old days, when the deafening whine of the chainsaw didn't yet exist and work was still performed by the sweat of a man's brow and the strength of his arm. The world of Frau Holle at the bottom of the well, where the good always receive their due reward. Before I make myself breakfast, I bring the woodcutter a cup of coffee and admire the wall of stacked wooden blocks. Enough to keep my home warm for several winters to come. And with the smaller twigs and branches he builds a mound where squirrels, birds and insects can find sanctuary. For him, this is a labour of love.

While he continues with his chopping, I think about what I have learnt from the karate master. If you want to chop through a brick with a single blow, you must not focus your thoughts on either the brick or the blow. Instead, you need to look further into the future, so that you can see beyond the blow. The karate master thinks that the brick is already broken before he hits it. This visualization of what will be: that is the hard work. The rest is a piece of cake.

And that's the way it is with everything you want to achieve in life: first visualize, then realize.

OSCAR VAN DEN BOOGAARD, *writer, in 'Wat wil je?' (What do you want), a column in* De Standaard, *a Belgian newspaper.*

2.
YOUR DREAM IS NOT (YET) CLEAR — WHAT THE HELP OF OTHERS CAN MEAN FOR ITS VISUALIZATION

Being able to follow the voice in your heart is not something that everyone can do. For some people, it is just not in their nature. Which is odd, if you consider that this is where your natural strength resides. Using that strength gives you energy, but first you have got to find it – and that can often be difficult. Very difficult. In my role as a coach – let's call it 'professional advisor in dream realization' – I frequently ask people how they see themselves in five, ten or twenty years' time. Some have a very clear vision of their future. Others find it less easy to visualize what lies ahead. Those who have accepted a status quo position for far too long are sometimes unaware of the strength of the fire, of the passion that lives inside them, of the potentially liberating effect of the voice in their heart. Bringing that fire, that passion and that voice to the surface is the first thing that needs to be done.

Having people around you who can see you as you really are, people who know you in your essence, helps to ensure that you can become the best and truest possible version of yourself. A supportive environment helps you tap the unbelievable power that lives inside you. Sometimes others catch a glimpse of your dream before you can see it yourself. 'I had the good fortune that my parents saw that I had a different talent than reading,' says Koen Vanmechelen. In this way, he underlines the crucial role played by others in freeing his dream and finding the tools that would allow its realization. Let Love Rule… You grow through the people who believe in you, who stick their neck out for you.

AT EXXONMOBIL I WAS THE FIRST ENGINEER EVER ALLOWED to lead an inspection team after just six months on the job. Unconsciously, I was aware that if I 'fell', my boss would be there to catch me. Just like my mum was there when I learnt to ride a bike as a child.

When the routine at ExxonMobil began to weigh me down, so that I began to hunger for something more – I live by constantly accepting new challenges – I left the company and moved to Kemira. I will never forget what my father said at the time. 'I don't really understand why you are leaving the richest company in the world to go and work with fertilizers. But if that is what makes you feel good, that's fine by me.'

The strength that grew inside me in this way made it possible later on for me to help others experience the same thing. I would like to tell you the story of **Robert.**

When I joined Kemira, it was as Head of the Purchasing and Logistics Department Benelux. For the first few days, I just walked around my department, introducing myself and trying to have a brief word with everyone. One of the people I met was Robert. At that time Robert was responsible for buying in raw materials for our Benelux factories. During our conversation I asked him how things were going. As an engineer, I was interested in the specifications he used for his purchasing, but Robert clearly had other things on his mind. He told me that his work no longer held much interest for him. It was clear that there was no 'fit' with who he was. Robert was the wrong man in the wrong place. His words gave me a funny feeling, but I carried on asking questions, probing deeper. 'Tell me, Robert, what did you do before?' His eyes began to sparkle and he told me about how he used to run the typing pool at Carbochimique. 'And what gave you so much pleasure in your work back then?' He answered in a flash, his voice full of passion and conviction: 'I was at the service of others. And I made sure that everything ran the way it was supposed to.' On my very first day at Kemira I decided that Robert and I would look together to see if we could find a solution for his problem.

Employees who are in the right place find their own drive. They also have a huge impact on the results of the departments where they work. Neither of these things was true in Robert's case. And so we tried to change that – together. At that time, Kemira had no internal vacancies. This meant we would have to try a different approach. Initially, Robert knew lots of things he didn't want to do, but found it hard to explain precisely what he did want to do.

In those days, I was not yet familiar with the concept of the WHY. But looking back now, I can see that the road Robert and I followed together was nothing less than the search for his WHY, the identification of his inner motivation, the unlocking of his dream. When we had clearly established what drove him, I began to look inside the organization for a set of tasks in which I knew he would shine.

The moment finally arrived when I thought I had found the perfect answer. I went to Robert and told him with some pride that I had arranged a job for him as Facility Manager. I had expected him to jump for joy. Instead, he gave me a whole list of reasons why he couldn't do it. He just wasn't the right person, he said. At this juncture, it was only my belief in Robert that allowed us to move forward. I looked at him and told him with confidence: 'Robert, you can do this.' I was thinking of the words that a CEO had once spoken to me: 'I push my people over the edge of the cliff, because I know they can fly.' To which I like to add: 'And if they fall, I am there to catch them.'

Robert duly became Facility Manager for the Benelux and some years later retired from the company as a happy man. In his farewell speech, he referred to his career switch as a key turning point...

For all of us, meeting others can be moments of life-changing importance. They can initiate the transitions that push our lives in this or that direction. None of us can survive without meetings of this kind. No-one can achieve their dream alone. Just as it takes a village to raise a child, so it often takes a whole community of people to make possible the realization of individual dreams. What's more, every fulfilling dream also contains a little something 'for the other'. Egocentric dreams may give you pleasure for a while, but if you want to fill an entire phase of your life with your dream, the way it connects you to others is one of its most crucial aspects.

WHAT I DID FOR ROBERT WAS BASED ON MY INTUITION. At the time, I did not yet know my own WHY. I still had no theoretical knowledge about transitions and human processes. Even so, I still felt a huge sense of satisfaction. I had succeeded in guiding someone to a job that suited him to perfection, a job that gave him energy, but also moved the organization closer to attaining its higher goals. I came to realize that it was important to map out areas in the company where positive results could be achieved. Much more important than trying to define the 'necessary functions' and who might best be able to fill them. Functions need to be fitted to people, not people to functions. My knowledge of my people turned out to be the second golden key to success. I understood their ambitions and motives. I knew what made them tick. I became less interested in how *things* are fitted together and more concerned about how *people* are fitted together. I gradually came to realize that what had given me most satisfaction throughout my working career was 'inspiring people to rise above themselves'. But it would still take a few more years before I realized that I had also found my own WHY!

Five years ago – in the meantime I had followed the necessary studies, courses and practical training – I set up TRAJECTUM, my own company, to provide transition guidance to individuals and organizations (people and systems). I had finally decided what I wanted to do. Based on my experience, a focus on results and a caring attitude towards others, from now on my aim would be to help people to realize their dreams and help organizations to make room for their people's dreams. More than ever, the world needs trust and passion. Or as Lenny Kravitz put it with such power and simplicity in his 2015 film of the same title: *Just Let Go*. 'Just let your people go' is perhaps the most powerful piece of advice I can give to anyone who is the leader of anything in this day and age. My work in TRAJECTUM supports me in my conviction that a dream job really does exist for everyone. We know that people operate within systems and that the nature of these systems is determined by those in the highest hierarchical positions. Surely in these circumstances it benefits us all if it is possible to work in an environment where giving trust and letting go are core elements.

3.
YOUR DREAM IS NOT (YET) CLEAR — HOW YOU CAN START TO VISUALIZE IT FOR YOURSELF

People who are connected to their WHY can see their dream and can inspire their environment to act. And people who are able to realize their dream in line with their WHY inspire others in their environment to do the same. The world has every interest in helping as many people as possible to see and fulfil their dream. Have you not yet progressed so far? Then it is high time for you to go in search of your WHY.

It is generally accepted that you will find it more quickly with a guide. Other people can help you to find the right way. This is what I try to do – and I like to do it under the watchful eye of Simon Sinek. Marketing consultant Simon Sinek studied cultural anthropology. In 2002, he started his own company. He became world famous with his TED talk *Start with why – how great leaders inspire action.* Starting from the idea that whatever is inspirational will automatically spread and with little more to help him than a powerful social network, supported by his books *Start with Why, Leaders Eat Last, Together is Better* and finally *Find your Why,* he succeeded in just a few years' time in sharing his story each day with an exponentially increasing number of inspired people and future inspirers. The genuine and infectious manner in which he was able to build up a community of happy employees and employers had a magnetic attraction that compelled others to follow. Sinek reduces his ideas about inspirational leadership and how to achieve it to their essence. As a result, they have the potential to radically change the direction of all our lives, both in a professional context and beyond.

> I HOPE TO INSPIRE OTHERS TO DO THE THINGS THAT INSPIRE THEM, SO THAT TOGETHER WE MIGHT BUILD THE COMPANIES, THE ECONOMY AND A WORLD IN WHICH TRUST AND LOYALTY ARE THE NORM AND NOT THE EXCEPTION. **SIMON SINEK**

How do you arrive at your dream? How do you know what inspires you? You do it with a compass in your pocket, a filter in your hand and in full awareness of your natural strength or core: your WHY. Having a clear view of your WHY is indispensible to realizing your dream.

> WHEN I SAY 'WHY', I DON'T MEAN TO MAKE MONEY — THAT'S A RESULT. BY 'WHY' I MEAN WHAT IS YOUR PURPOSE, CAUSE OR BELIEF? 'WHY' DOES YOUR COMPANY EXIST? 'WHY' DO YOU GET OUT OF BED EVERY MORNING? AND 'WHY' SHOULD ANYONE CARE?
> **SIMON SINEK**

As an adult, you get up each morning to earn money and pay the bills. But is that the only reason? Is there nothing more? Of course there is! Earning money is no more than the result of what you do. You don't get out of bed each morning to earn money. You get out of bed each morning to do something.

And why do you do what you do? Why do I write a book and do you build a house? Why did I become an engineer and you become a nurse? Why do I now coach groups and individuals while you work as an entrepreneur?

> GREAT LEADERS ARE THOSE WHO TRUST THEIR GUT. THEY ARE THOSE WHO UNDERSTAND THE ART BEFORE THE SCIENCE. THEY WIN HEARTS BEFORE MINDS. THEY ARE THE ONES WHO START WITH 'WHY'. **SIMON SINEK**

According to Simon Sinek, the charisma of all 'great leaders' – the kind of people who you sense are at one with their inner strength, who show that what they are doing perfectly matches who they are, so that you follow them because you want to and not because you have to – is the result of just one thing: great leaders have a crystal-clear vision of their own WHY. The motives that drive them are visible at all times, not only to themselves but also to others. When great leaders communicate, they always begin with the story of their own WHY.

In the early 1900s, Samuel Pierpont Langley worked to develop the very first aeroplane. In this venture, he had the support of the relevant government authorities, as well as adequate manpower and financial resources. A few hundred kilometres away Wilbur and Orville Wright were also trying to develop an aeroplane. They had none of the contacts, subsidies and state support on which Langley could rely. What they did have was the enthusiasm and commitment of a handful of dedicated people in their home town. None of the people in their team were professionally trained. Nor were the brothers themselves. But they had a passion to be the first to fly. In a bicycle repair workshop, they worked night and day at the realization of their dream. On 17 December 1903, a small group of men and women stood on a hillside in Kittyhawk, North Carolina, to watch mankind's first-ever powered flight, piloted by a member of the Wright brothers' team.

Why did Wilbur and Orville Wright succeed where Samuel Pierpont Langley – who had better equipment, greater financial backing and a more highly trained team of experts – failed? Was it just a matter of luck? Not at all. The Wright brothers and Langley were both highly motivated. Both teams had an almost obsessive work ethic, supported by the sharpest academic minds in the field. They both had exactly the same dream. But it was only the Wright brothers who were able to inspire their entourage to commit themselves 100% and more to the development of a technology they fervently believed would change the world. The Wright brothers began with... WHY.

Knowing your WHY helps you first to see your dream and then to realize it. Your WHY serves as a compass in your search, as a filter to select the things that best suit you, as a yardstick for taking decisions, as a gentle push to take that step you have been wanting to take for so long, but never dared – until now. Knowing your WHY leads you through all trials and tribulations, until you arrive safely at the place where you want to be. Men and women who know why they do what they do experience feelings of self-confidence, calm, balance, happiness, energy and enjoyment. No dream is impossible for people with a clear WHY. Or as we say jokingly in our office: 'Where there's a WHY, there's a way!' Joking aside, if you know why you want what you want, the universe will conspire to help you. And to make it even better still:

> THE POWER OF 'WHY' IS NOT OPINION.
> IT'S BIOLOGY. **SIMON SINEK**

It works like this. In Simon Sinek's model three concentric circles revolve around each other, which he refers to as the 'golden circle' of WHY, HOW and WHAT. In the WHY you can recognize what I call your core, the essence of who you are. Together, the HOW, which contains your talents and identity, and the WHY form your filter or compass. The WHAT is what you depict when you finally start working on the painting of your life from the starting point of 'I see myself as...'

By a neat natural coincidence, this is also how the human brain is organized. The outer circle is our linguistic Homo sapiens brain or neocortex. This is responsible for our rational and analytical thinking. Inside that is the limbic brain or system, which is non-linguistic and governs our feelings and human behaviour. Our decisions are also directed by the limbic brain: trust is developed by whatever is consistent and agrees with what we believe. This explains why we prefer to use the 14-year-old daughter of our next door neighbour as our babysitter rather than the 35-year-old (and well qualified) child carer who has just moved into our street. We know the girl, but we have never met the woman. The former has therefore had the chance to develop our trust, whereas the latter has so far been denied the opportunity (as it were) to work on our limbic brain. Facts, figures and hard evidence are never enough to override a feeling of trust that someone or something gives. Or doesn't.

But what if something prevents you from finding your WHY? What if the path leading you towards it is blocked? We are often not aware of it, but we all grew up surrounded by numerous dominating influences. Many of these influences are fears, and together they help to make us who we are. This is what we call nurture.

As a Jungian analyst, Willem de Jager has worked for the last fifteen years to develop an instrumentarium that helps to guide people through their efforts to understand their (subconscious) motives and their behavior. With his Odin Company, he has devised a revolutionary psychometric assessment tool: the Odin Development Compass (ODC).

The ODC is a unique measurement instrument that offers people self-insight and identifies in a well-grounded way the sources of their natural strength. It does this by mapping out which behaviour gives you energy and which behaviour costs you energy. It also makes a distinction between your developable talent (your natural development potential), your vulnerable strength (learnt behaviour, which can be distorted under pressure into less effective or even counter-productive behaviour), and, finally, an unknown zone (which is the repository of the things you are naturally less good at and therefore avoid doing). You should keep away from this last zone: no matter how hard you try, you can never develop the things it contains into a natural and successful strength.

Willem: *'What I have developed is a model to identify complexes, a model that will allow you to draw out the shadows that guide you but that you no longer know from the dark places in your mind where you have hidden them. People sometimes fail to understand why they behave the way they do. I am thinking, for example, of a politician who can only communicate through shouting, so that he constantly creates the opposite effect to what he intends. Or a brilliant musician who fails to find a way to turn his passion into a professional career, even though on the surface he seems to possess all the qualities that are necessary to make this possible. Of course, there are also people who have become isolated from who they really are as a result of a traumatic experience in their past. Fortunately, this is often not so serious that it is not possible to still give them a clear insight into the things they are good at and like to do. In other words, the things that can lead you directly to your dream.*

My personal passion is to ensure that people have a clear view of all the many different things that are projected onto and into them in the course of their life. "If we could teach our children to come to terms with our projections, there would be no more wars," says James Hillman in his book The Code of the Soul. *I wouldn't go as far as that. But what I do know is that the only way to achieve satisfaction in life is through authentic dreaming, in balance with yourself. There is no such thing as a "recipe for success". The reason why Steve Jobs devoted so much attention to the unseen parts of the devices he brought to market was connected entirely with the fact that his father was a fence-builder. For him, the back of the fence had to be as attractive as the front. Working with the same kind of mentality was important for Steve when he started his own business. It was part of who he was. Sadly, this is not transposable!'*

Where are you on the scale of 'Dreaming & Executing'? Have a look at trajectum.be/thebook to find out all you need to know.

Fertility comes from the outside.

KOEN VANMECHELEN

‘It is life itself, the freedom that the artist experiences which makes him look forward time after time to whatever will emerge from the egg. The desire to cross-fertilize has taken root in him as a dream – DREAM – from the outside.’

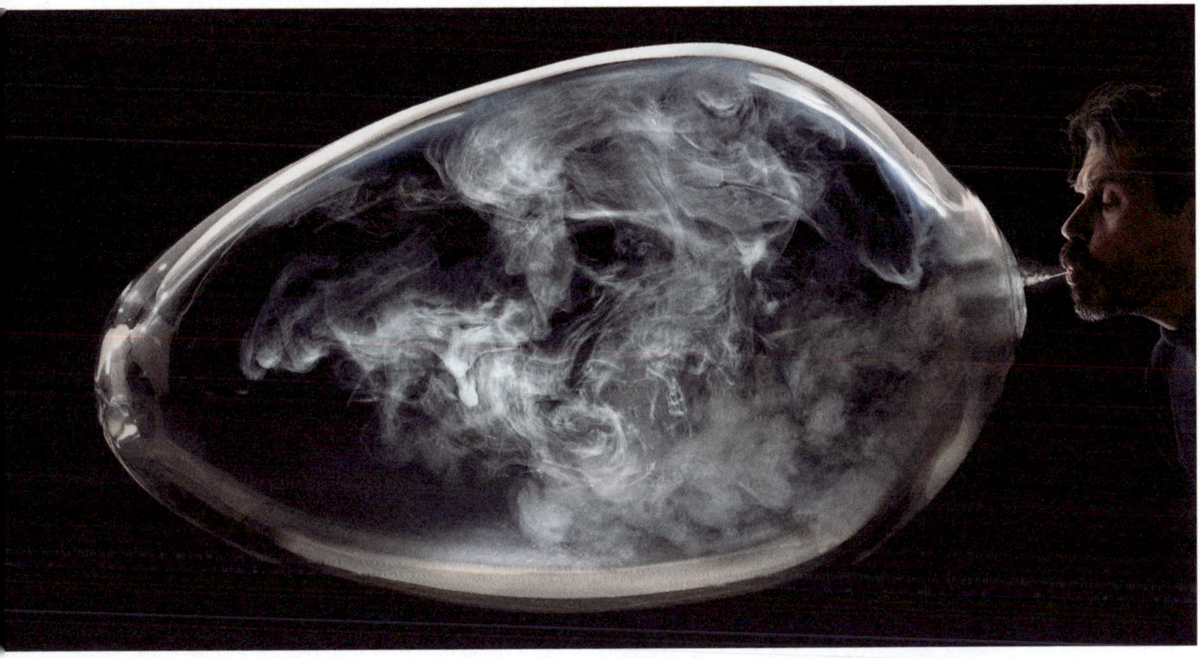

bulence © KOEN VANMECHELEN, 2016

HOW TO PRACTICE 'DREAMING'

*It was one of those afternoons when **my mother,** who was a nursery school teacher, brought her entire class to our house, so that the children could enjoy playing in the garden. The blacksmith was also there, attending to our horses' hooves. When it was time to go back to school, the smith watched in amazement as my mum gathered together her 'flock' with seeming ease. 'But madam,' he asked, 'how are you able to deal with so many children all at the same time? I wouldn't know where to begin.' My mother laughed, gave him a knowing look, and answered. 'But Mark, I wouldn't be able to do what you do, either!'*

How can you visualize your dream?

Your dream lives deep inside you. If you want to visualize it – which is the first step on the way to its realization – you need to look deep into your inner self. First look for your HOW and only then for your WHY. Your dream will become visible in each image, in every WHAT that you subsequently depict in 'the painting of your life'.

Look for the two elements of your HOW:

1 your unique talent: As well as a wide range of skills, you also have a single unique talent. To find out what it is, you need to ask yourself and others:
  - what do you really love doing and what are you super-good at;
  - what never makes you tired, but actually makes you shine;
  - what always gives you energy and never takes it away;
  - what things strike you as important, even when you were young;
  - what do you never postpone or make an excuse to avoid;
  - what gives you a feeling of total success, deep satisfaction and real happiness;

– what makes you forget everything else when you are doing it: no hunger, thirst, tiredness or boredom, just a deep sense of inner peace and a fire that burns inside you, so that you feel as though you can take on the entire world?

My unique talent is 'connecting people'. What's yours?

2 your identity
– What values are important to you?
– What 'label' do you want to wear?
– What can someone else make you feel responsible for?
– When do you correct yourself? What for?

My identity: 'enthusiastic', 'result-oriented' and 'connective'. What's yours?

Search for your WHY or your mission, the things for which you engage your HOW:

your mission
– a combination of your talents and your values
– your life's work or objective
– your contribution to society, what you want to be remembered by...

My mission is 'to inspire people to rise above themselves'. What's yours?

The following two exercises can help you to find clarity about your dream:

1 'The 40-year vision'

Ask yourself what you would see if you had a crystal ball that could show you your life in 5, 10, 20, 30 or 40 years' time. How would things be different? Would you still be in a relationship? What relationship? How would your relations with your family have changed? Who would be your friends? What would you do together? Where would you live? How financially secure would you be? What would your health be like? Will you live life at a hundred miles an hour or will you just breeze through life at a gentle pace?

This exercise need not last longer than an hour. Give your unconscious free rein. Imagine wonderful things for yourself. Does it all look very different from your life now? It does? Now you can see just how far you still have to go before you can reach your dream. So don't wait until it is too late. Make time to listen to the voice of your heart!

2 'The 7 stories'

What were the most enriching experiences in your life?

Try to remember things you did really well or enjoyed enormously. It doesn't matter what other people think about these things. And it is not important whether you were paid for doing them or not. Time and place are equally irrelevant. All that counts is that they made you feel happy; that you thought you had succeeded brilliantly; that you believed you had achieved something.

This exercise usually takes a couple of days to complete. Make a list of at least 25 personal or professional experiences that meet the above criteria. Write down everything that comes into your mind, no matter how simple or straightforward it might seem. Think of concrete examples, situations or tasks, not skills or capabilities. For example: I acted in a play, I organized a youth tournament, I travelled through Africa, etc. Not: I am artistic, I can run things, I like travelling, etc. From your list of 25 choose the seven experiences that gave you most pleasure and/or the greatest sense of achievement. Set them in order of priority from one to seven. For each of the seven, ask yourself precisely what you did by answering questions like: What was the most important aspect of what you did? What did you enjoy the most/least? What was your task? What was your main motivation? What was your role? What problems did you face? How did you solve them? In what kind of environment did this experience take place?

Are there common factors running through the seven stories you describe? Which elements keep recurring? The answer to these questions is your WHY or your mission: a verb (your contribution)... so that... (your impact).

The standard work for anyone who wants to find the core of their dream:

Sinek, S. (2017). *Find your Why.* London: Penguin Books.

People who know their WHY, who know 'what makes the heart rejoice', are already in the starting blocks for the race that leads to the realization of their dream. People who know their WHY possess the necessary tools to be the architect of their own lives.

STAND,

There are no words to describe what moves a spider to repair the damage to its web with imperturbable concentration. Words are a distraction that spiders do not use to make clear the things that are occupying their attention. The web is their only language, just like branches are the language of a tree and rain the language of a storm cloud. (...)

People need words. With their heads full of turbulent thoughts, they search for ways to make clear what is happening inside them. The conversations and writings with which they swamp each other are word-rivers on which their thoughts float.

But what do they mean? Do people understand each other if they address each other in words alone?

GERARD BODIFEE, *astrophysicist, philosopher, writer and columnist, in* De Standaard *newspaper*

STAND UP, SPEAK OUT LOUD THE DREAM THAT LIVES INSIDE YOU

SEEING YOUR DREAM IS NOT ENOUGH. TO REALLY START MOVING TOWARDS IT, YOU MUST DARE TO SPEAK OUT LOUD AND SAY WHAT IT IS!

The core of your dream has now been defined. Your WHY no longer holds any secrets for you. There is nothing to prevent you from starting the painting of your life. The road is open. You are capable of visualizing your dream. It is time to take it to the stage! You must stand and put your dream into words. You must speak it out loud, talk about it, make it tangible, not just for yourself but for everyone around you. Make sure that you are listened to. Don't be afraid. Make your presence felt and you will soon see that there are people who are ready to help you, who are prepared to work with you to build your dream. It is not only when searching for your dream that others are important. You also need others when you stand up to announce your dream. And you will continue to need them, right from your dream's first expression until its final completion.

AN EARLY MORNING, 8 O'CLOCK, KEMIRA HEAD OFFICE, HELSINKI, FINLAND. It is November 2003. I am the COO in charge of the Speciality Crop Care business unit. A 180-million-euro global speciality fertilizer business with assets in EMEA and Asia. This business unit – the result of a strategic exercise of which I was part – was launched in January 2000. That morning in Helsinki I had been on the job for almost four years. I was with the unit right from the very start and was involved in all its subsequent worldwide acquisitions. I had made all the choices relating to distribution and taken all the decisions about joint ventures.

The CEO called me to his office and asked me to close the door. He told me of the decision the Kemira board had taken to terminate its fertilizer activities. Other commodity fertilizers would be floated on the stock market but our business unit was insufficiently prepared for this. The unit would therefore be converted into a stand alone company and sold off. This would also be my last project for the company. So there I was. What should I do? Accept the task? Or bow out and leave it to someone else?

I promised the CEO that I would return the next morning at 8 o'clock with an answer. For the rest of the day I worked my way diligently through my 'to-do' list and in the evening went for a long walk along the coast. There was no one I could call. No one I could confide in. All I had was my own inner voice, my personal compass. I decided that I would do what the company asked – and for two reasons. First, during my studies I had only learnt about acquiring companies, but never about companies that were destined to close down. Of course, I had heard the terrible stories about the impact such decisions can have on employees, customers and suppliers, but I wanted to accept the challenge and see for myself. Second, I wanted to show that our team was strong enough to do this; that we were not afraid to move into uncharted waters. And so the next day I told the CEO that I would take on the task, but only on two conditions. Condition no. 1: I needed to be kept fully informed, including everything that was happening at board level with relevance for the sale. Condition no. 2: my salary would be doubled, based on objectives set by the CEO each year – no cure, no pay.

My proposal was accepted. In the days that followed, I searched feverishly for ways to consolidate the unit's safe and well-anchored basis that I had helped to create, so that it would come through the sale process intact. My main concern was to avoid reaching the finish line with a group of disjointed and dispirited ex-employees. My main fear was that the images I had in my mind about the way they might be treated – or rather mistreated, with a lack of human decency, respect and proper guidance – could be true.

I was determined not to let it happen like that. I would shepherd my people with care and consideration to our parting of the ways. I would preserve and further stimulate their self-directing abilities, even in these difficult circumstances. Above all, I would help to build for each of them a vision of the future that would help to dispel the paralyzing fear that so often accompanies situations of this kind. In short, I wanted to help each of them to find their dream, so that when the unit closed down they could set off on the right path to search for something new.

I am as convinced as I was back then that nothing inevitably needs to happen 'the way it always does'. It is possible at every moment in your life to decide that this time things can be done differently. All you need is belief in yourself and belief in where you are going. Plenty of effort, trust and working together with others also help. As does giving verbal expression to your needs. Like in Lenny Kravitz's song: 'Stand'...

LENNY KRAVITZ. *Stand*

Don't give up,
You're gonna see tomorrow
That you'll be on your feet again
Sometimes the world's gonna knock you over
But you will see who are your friends

Come on, stand, up again
Come on, stand,
Stand, you're gonna run again

Your faith and patience will be your soldiers
To guide you through your troubled times
Just put one foot in front of the other
The battles are inside your mind
You have the power to face your demons
No matter how they go at time
And rid yourself of your fear and weakness
So you can start to live your life

Pick up your will
And put on your face
If you need to, just take my hand
It's time to demonstrate, don't hesitate
Just get up and say 'Yes, I can'

Stand, you're gonna run again
Stand, you're gonna run again

A degree of caution is needed when giving feedback to someone who is in the early stages of formulating his/her dream. Think carefully about this when you are listening to other people's hopes and aspirations. Remember that words can sometimes wound. You don't want to be responsible for someone giving up their dream, do you? 'Man's deadliest weapon is language,' said the Anglo-Hungarian philosopher and engineer Arthur Koestler (1905-1983). The Arabs also have a memorable saying that expresses much the same sentiment: 'Three things never return: a word that has been spoken, an arrow that has been shot and a chance that has not been taken.' So don't forget: you have something precious in your hands when someone entrusts their dream to you. Make sure you are worthy of that trust!

Remember also that before people can find the words to express their dream, they sometimes need someone or something to give them a bit of a push. It is almost as if they need to be 'invited' to leave their comfort zone. In some cases, a 'little bit of pain' can also help. Sometimes even a lot of pain may be necessary.

What will give you the strength and the courage to put your dream into words? What can help you speak out to the world, so that others can help you in your quest? What do you need and how can this book support you along the way?

Just as we called on Simon Sinek to help us visualize our dream, we are now going to turn to George Kohlrieser for advice about the best way to formulate that dream in language that everyone can understand. As well as being the author of *Hostage at the Table* and *Care to Dare,* George Kohlrieser is professor of leadership and organizational behaviour at the IMD Business School in Lausanne. In the past, he has also worked as a successful hostage negotiator. It is from this perspective that he views leadership development. According to his theory, people all too often allow themselves to be taken hostage by their own thoughts and experiences (influenced by their attachment style) or by the behaviour of others. As a result, we frequently see threats but ignore possibilities. It is almost as if you are a metaphorical hostage in your own life. And indeed, whenever you feel hemmed in, powerless or vulnerable, you are truly no better than a hostage.

> THE ANTIDOTE TO POWERLESSNESS IS EMOTIONAL BONDING. BY CONNECTING TO PEOPLE OR GOALS, WE CAN CREATE BONDS THAT ENABLE US TO FEEL EMPOWERED. BONDING IS A SURVIVAL MECHANISM FOR US ALL. THROUGH BONDING, WE ENRICH OUR LIVES.
> **GEORGE KOHLRIESER**

Kohlrieser attaches great importance to searching for contact and connections with others. He speaks about the crucial impact of the 'bonding circle' on the development of trust and confidence. Difficult situations arise from a failure to follow this circle correctly. But making sure you have 'secure bases' can help you to avoid this mistake.

Self-leadership – which for me is the sum of self-knowledge, self-control and self-motivation – is the alpha and omega for the realization of a dream. Knowing your WHY has helped you to visualize your dream. Having a clear view of your secure bases and your attachment style can now help you to give that dream shape and form in words.

1.
THE IMPORTANCE OF 'SECURE BASES'

It is good to be a house
for the only heart
you do not want to leave behind.
It is good to be a ladder
for children
who on a sombre day
want to climb towards the sun.
It is good to be a door,
softly creaking but still opening
for all who wish to enter.
And a window
in which the light never goes out
for all who think:
it is already late.

VJATSJELAV KOEPRIJANOV, *poet*

On our path through life we all come across people who inspire us; who play an important role in defining how we see ourselves; who sometimes even have the power to change us. These are our 'secure bases': men and women who challenge us to reach goals that we never imagined were possible, providing us with a framework for success but never intervening unless it is absolutely necessary. They push open the door that leads to our WHY. They show us how to find the strength we experience when what we do and what we say is perfectly aligned with what we feel and what we stand for as a person. They offer us opportunities to tap the potential that lies deep in all of us. In short, they give us the courage we need to speak out, to dare to express our dream to the world.

IN MY LIFE, WHICH HAS ALREADY LASTED FOR MORE THAN HALF A CENTURY, I have been inspired by a number of such 'leaders': my mother and later also my sister, a teacher in primary school, two teachers in secondary school, and three business leaders. 'Hold your head high! Stand up for yourself, but always in a respectful manner.' This was the lesson pumped into me at home. A second lesson I learnt from my secure bases was that as a woman I should always be able to make my own way and take responsibility for my own actions. The assertiveness and the resilience of this basic philosophy have helped me in many difficult situations.

Like the time when I had just started at Kemira. I had an appointment to see my brand-new boss, but when I arrived at the appointed time, his office was empty. Not wishing to waste my time with waiting when I had no idea how long he would be away, I left him a brief note: 'I was here at 2 pm, as we agreed. I will be in my office if you need me.' After that, I never had to wait for my boss again. Nor did my colleagues.

In the same context – we are still going back a few years – my visit to the ExxonMobil stand at a job fair in the late 1980s still remains fresh in my memory. 'You probably don't recruit women, do you?' was my (admittedly provocative) opener. 'Oh yes, of course we do' was the reply. During the following weeks I was subjected to no fewer than nine in-depth interviews. Everything went well, until the final question of the final interview: 'Are you planning to get married and have children?' I answered in all honesty that for the time being I had no real idea or plans in that direction. Even so, I immediately had the impression that from that moment on things were turning against me. I was afraid that they would reject me and that their so-called willingness to give women a fair chance was – as I had suspected from the start – no more than politically correct window dressing. When the interview was over, the head of the panel rose to his feet and quickly pulled on his coat. As he left, I heard him say to a colleague: 'Must dash. I've got to get home to the wife and kids...'

‘Hmm,’ I thought. Maybe the situation wasn’t so negative after all. There was one way to find out. I walked over to him, looked him straight in the eye and said in a firm voice: ‘Yes, everyone has different roles in life don’t they?’ I knew as I said it that this had probably ruined my chances for good, but I was convinced that right was on my side. And it felt good. The next day, I received a telephone call to tell me that I had got the job. I could start at the production unit in Meerhout, where I was made responsible for machines that made polyethylene pellets at a high pressure of 2,500-3,000 Bar.

Here’s another example. Less than three weeks after starting at Exxon-Mobil I went to a weekend concert in Paris organized by Amnesty International. Bruce Springsteen was one of the artists. At the time, I was a young twenty-something and Springsteen was an icon. After the concert, I bought a poster of the man himself, with which I intended to brighten up my chic but otherwise extremely boring office. Even though I hadn’t picked up any warning signals in advance, it soon became clear that I had created some kind of culture shock within the company. People giggled, pointed, tutted or simply shook their heads in silence. I was puzzled, but still didn’t realize that I had done anything wrong. Until one day my secretary closed the office door behind her, pointed at the poster and said: ‘Hilde, you don’t know what you have done, do you? Daring to hang up a poster like that here! No one’s ever seen anything like it! You’re the original bull in a china shop. But please: don’t change!’

In none of the above examples was it ever my intention to shock or provoke. I was not trying to make a statement. I was just being myself. But because the things I expressed – symbolically or not – were in keeping with what I felt and what I stood for, I was never punished for what might have been interpreted by more malicious people as a form of rebellion. Even today, I still believe that if your intentions are good and you choose your words carefully, there is a good chance you can gain acceptance for a different opinion or behaviour that varies from the norm.

'Hilde, I am always going to tell you what I think, even though I know you don't always want to hear it.'
My mother

Strange as it might sound, you can compare secure bases with cycling! 'Life,' I have heard my mother say for as long as I can remember, 'is like riding a bike. You first have to learn how to do it. Then you have to keep on pedalling. Sometimes the wind will be against you, sometimes at your back. Sometimes you have to climb hard uphill, sometimes you can free-wheel down the other side. When things are tough, it's good to know that other cyclists will be on the same road, encouraging you to get to the top. They give you wings, help to carry you, so that you can rest a little. Just like you, when you are feeling stronger, can be a support for others.'

You probably don't stop to think about it too often, but you almost certainly have secure bases in your life as well. They are like anchors, the foundations on which you can build, the source of your courage and energy to speak out. Your secure bases give you comfort and protection. They make it possible for you to lower your defences, offering space for imagination and creativity. Realizing a dream means doing something that has not been done before. In other words, something new. You can only be innovative in places where trust is present, where people take care of you, where you can experiment without any guarantee of success, safe in the knowledge that you will be given a second chance if things don't turn out as planned. People who want to stand up and speak out their dreams need secure bases.

> WITHOUT SECURE BASES WE BECOME PRONE TO ANXIETY OR FEAR, THUS LIMITING OUR POTENTIAL, HINDERING SUCCESS AND MAKING US LIABLE TO BECOME A HOSTAGE, EITHER OF OURSELVES OR OF CERTAIN EVENTS IN OUR LIFE. **GEORGE KOHLRIESER**

Koen Vanmechelen: *'Sometimes I have been a long way away. How did I get back? That's not difficult to answer: through love. Love gives you energy and shows you which way to go. When you are always searching for new frontiers, you often end up in no-man's-land. That's when you need to be surrounded by people who care. Otherwise, you can quickly get lost. There needs to be someone to tell you it's okay. That what you are doing is good.'*

The most obvious form of a secure base is a person. Often, your earliest secure bases are found close to home: parents, grandparents, brothers and sisters, other members of the family, friends... Later on, people in your professional life can also become secure bases: a coach, a mentor, a leader, a supervisor, a boss. But it doesn't stop there. You can also have more distant secure bases: a film star you admire (you don't have to have met him or her), a doctor, a therapist. Being a secure base for someone does not necessarily imply action or interaction. This applies equally to the secure bases that are not person-based. Goals, places and objects can also serve as secure bases. They offer the feeling of security that you need if you want to grow. They give you the confidence to take steps and accept challenges. The concept of secure bases helps us, as people, to organize and give meaning to our thoughts, emotions and experiences.

> BONDING IS A PRIMARY NEED, JUST LIKE AIR, FOOD AND WATER. IT IS THE FOUNDATION OF ENDURING SUCCESS FOR PEOPLE AND ORGANIZATIONS.
> THE CYCLE OF BONDING – ATTACHMENT, BONDING, SEPARATION, GRIEVING – IS A NATURAL PART OF LIFE THAT WE REPEATEDLY GO THROUGH. WHEN PEOPLE BECOME STUCK IN SEPARATION AND GRIEF, THEY CAN BECOME HOSTAGES TO THEMSELVES AND OTHERS.
> SAYING GOODBYE IS A NECESSARY PATH TO MAKING NEW BONDS AND FINDING THE JOY OF LIFE AGAIN.
> **GEORGE KOHLRIESER**

***Isis** grew up as an only child in a nest where security and care were often hard to find. She lived with her mother, who at different phases of Isis's childhood was wrestling with demons of her own, a fight that more often than not she lost. From time to time, one of the step-fathers who occasionally sailed across the horizon of Isis's young life would provide a degree of temporary stability, but she found her greatest sense of security among her friends at school and later in a few 'good lovers'. She was blond, easy to be with and laughed a lot. A frivolous child, perhaps, who during puberty gained a little extra credibility with her peers through her stories about her fragile domestic environment. When she was fourteen, she moved from the 'provincial' town of Kortrijk to the 'big city' of Antwerp. This gave her already independent lifestyle a new boost. She did her best at school and filled every spare moment of her day with reading. This made it possible for her to escape inside her own mind – books as secure bases – allowing her to keep her head above water in the pool of misery to which she was daily forced to return.*

After her studies, and following a brief passage through the world of publishing, she eventually ended up as a 'performer' in the circus that is politics. The non-stop pressure, the constant need to counter bad news, the obligation to deal with huge super-egos: all these things drove her further and further away from the deepest core of who she was.

The turning point in Isis's life came after a relaxing massage one evening. It was there that she first came into contact with yoga. Daring to listen in silence and with full concentration to what her body wanted to tell her had a wonderfully liberating effect. It opened up a whole new world, which initially gave her more satisfaction than all the knowledge and wisdom in all the books she had ever read, which until then had been her 'salvation'. She started to train as a yoga teacher and gave free lessons to people from her neighbourhood in her own home. The trust and appreciation this brought her, together with the support she received from her partner, provided her with new secure bases. But this time they were secure bases that perfectly matched the deepest drivers in her life. Filled with new confidence and encouraged by those around her, she decided to set up her own yoga and massage studio. She specialized in mindfulness, children's yoga, pre-natal yoga and embodiment. And before she knew it, business was booming.

In her lessons she places an emphasis on first consciously learning to feel your body, as a precursor to consciously working on your mind. Through introspection and insight, but sprinkled with a liberal dose of humour and pleasure, she paves the way for bonding – both she with her trainees and the trainees with their own inner selves. The sense of security that comes from being at one with your own body and the mental resilience this creates: these are the things that Isis wants to pass on to as many people as possible, especially children.

Today, Isis lives in full connection with her own WHY. She seeks to give people the same security that she was only able to find relatively late in life, and this through the instrument of their own body and the way it works. Isis: 'Over the years, the strength that emanates from this deeper way of feeling has led to stability and acceptance in my own life, also as far as my parents are concerned. I know that both my parents love me. It was just that life made it difficult from them to show this love in the right way.'

This same strength now forms the basis for the love that is making the bond between mother and daughter grow a little bit stronger each day.

> OFTEN, THOSE INDIVIDUALS WHO MAKE THE DEEPEST ATTACHMENTS TO PEOPLE OR GOALS, WHO ARE THE MOST SUCCESSFUL OR HAPPY, ARE THOSE WHO HAVE KNOWN THE DEEPEST MOMENTS OF STRUGGLE.
> **GEORGE KOHLRIESER**

If you feel safe and secure, you dare to share the things that truly matter to you. In short, you dare to speak your dream out loud. But before you can reach this stage, you first need to confront your own loss experiences.

It is only when you can recognize the existence of these experiences that you can make further progress in the cycle of bonding. Only then can you gradually process the loss and give it a place. When this happens, you will be ready to make new attachments, to trust people again and take them into your confidence, and to set new objectives for yourself. In this way, a new cycle of bonding is initiated.

> WITHOUT GOOD SECURE BASES, THE INDIVIDUAL IS LEFT TO THE PRIMAL FLIGHT-FIGHT REFLEXES. SECURE BASES HAVE THE POWER TO INFLUENCE WHETHER OR NOT WE BECOME HOSTAGES TO OURSELVES OR TO EVENTS IN OUR LIVES.
> **GEORGE KOHLRIESER**

To make attachment and bonding possible, we therefore need safety and trust. In addition to being based on observation, this necessity can also be seen in human biology. If we are in an environment that offers us neither safety nor trust, the body releases the hormone cortisol – also known as the alertness hormone – to protect us. This in turn releases additional adrenaline that gives us strength and energy to either stay and face the possible danger (fight) or to run away (flight). A high level of cortisol in the body also reduces the level of oxytocine (the cuddle hormone). And a low level of oxytocine means that we are less inclined to trust people, so that we are less inclined to work with them to overcome difficulties or solve problem. Not exactly ideal circumstances in which to realize your dream. The burden is too great, your ability to shoulder it too inadequate. As a result, you feel stress.

Claude Heninger was a flying instructor attached to a training school at Lausanne airport in Switzerland. In January 2001, he took off for a lesson with a pupil who already had 1,300 hours of flying experience. During take-off one of the wheels lost its locking pin. Claude was already in the air before he realized that the plane would have to land without a properly functioning undercarriage. Claude's first thought was to take over the controls from his pupil and land himself. But he almost immediately had another idea. He asked the pupil a few questions to see how he was feeling, so that he could assess if he was sufficiently capable of flying and landing the plane himself in this emergency situation. The pupil confirmed that he was okay and was willing to bring the plane down. This gave Claude, in his role as supervisor, the opportunity to monitor the broader picture. The pupil then proceeded to complete the flight in safety, with his instructor at his side, offering advice and input where necessary.

When asked about the experience afterwards, Claude said that the most difficult thing for him was the need to relinquish control. It was hard for him to let go. But it was precisely through letting go that he was able to create space in which his pupil could grow.

Claude Heninger was for his pupil what George Kohlrieser calls a 'secure base leader'. He transferred to his pupil not only his knowledge, but also certain attitudes and even a high degree of power. A secure base leader is a self-leader who has matured into a leader of others. Because he is in full contact with the deepest core of his inner being, he is able to make room that allows the people around him – either his subordinates in an organization or others who feel inspired in a natural (non-institutionalized) manner to follow him – to undergo the same transformational process as himself. This, of course, creates a fertile environment for the development of a new crop of secure base leaders.

A secure base leader provides protection, safety and encouragement, whilst at the same time promoting exploration and the taking of 'healthy' risks. The authentic way in which he cares for those in his charge challenges them to dare. Above all, it challenges them to dare to dream – and then to pursue that dream.

Well-aligned people are self-leaders: secure base leaders, who are also sometimes known as 'care to dare' leaders. George Kohlrieser lists nine attitudes that characterize them: 1. they always remain calm; 2. they recognize each person as an individual; 3. they can see the potential in people; 4. they listen and inquire; 5. they excite and enthuse; 6. they focus on the positive; 7. they encourage the taking of risks; 8. they inspire using intrinsic motivation; 9. they exude accessibility. They are the leaders we all want. And we can be one ourselves!

In addition to mapping out your secure bases, it is also of crucial importance that your attachment style provides you with (or allows you to make) the safe environment where you can speak out your dream with confidence.

2.
THE INFLUENCE OF YOUR ATTACHMENT STYLE

The way you interact with others is determined to a significant degree by deep-rooted – and sometimes very rigid – patterns that are reflected in your attachment style. It has been shown that to a large extent this style is already developed during your childhood years. To make good contact with your inner self – an essential condition for being able to visualize and express your dream – you must have a clear insight into your (sometimes variable) attachment style.

Based on research by his respected colleagues and predecessors Eric Berne and Kim Bartholomew, George Kohlrieser devised a cross-shaped figure that depicts the four most important attachment styles. The four poles are formed by the idea that there are primarily two dimensions that play a role in the way that people think about their relations with others. These are the 'self-dimension' and the 'other dimension', each of which has a positive and a negative pole. The self-dimension reflects what we think and believe about ourselves (I am competent, I will succeed, I can do this). The other dimension reflects what we think and believe about other people (other people are to be trusted, other people will help me, I can rely on other people). Your attachment style in a given situation is the intersection between how you think about yourself and how you think about others. This results in four quadrants, one for each style of attachment.

> LEADERSHIP IS A SET OF BEHAVIOURS YOU LEARN, STARTING AS A CHILD AND CONTINUING THROUGHOUT YOUR LIFE. YOU CAN BREAK OLD PATTERNS AND BUILD NEW ONES. **GEORGE KOHLRIESER**

According to George Kohlrieser, the four most common attachment styles are the following:

1) the secure style: this style is focused on support, security, the provision of safety and trust, and the encouragement of risk-taking, discovery, creativity and learning; it is important that people who wish to continue functioning in this quadrant must work constantly at increasing their self-awareness and must make use of their secure bases as role models and a sounding-board;

2) the avoidant-dismissive style: this style is focused on control and is therefore dominant in nature; as such, it is adopted by many people in senior positions of leadership, who succeed in functioning in this quadrant for long periods of time; the main pitfalls of the style are a lack of trust in others and the absence of secure bases;

3) the anxious style: this style is focused on self-preservation, a need rooted in a negative self-image; people in this quadrant avoid risks to prevent harming their bonding with others; the learning process necessary to progress from this style to the secure style involves learning to trust yourself and your own judgement, without being too dependent on those around you;

4) the detached style: the proponents of this style often become confused by their emotions and lose control in stressful situations; it is almost as if they are a hostage to their feelings and so they hide inside their shell to protect themselves from harm; people in this quadrant are spectators in their own life story; to evolve in a more positive direction it is first necessary to learn how to bond with others.

Having insight into your own attachment style and the implications of the quadrant in which you are currently situated can help to make you more aware of your behaviour. You can then focus on developing new behaviour that brings you as close as possible to the secure style. This means that you will need to break through your usual pattern of behaviour. Effectively, you must be prepared to 'reprogramme' your brain. Remember, however, that you are still always a person of flesh and blood. Be kind to yourself during the change process. Having a bad day every once in a while is not the end of the world.

As soon as you are aware of your secure bases, you can strengthen them further. And as soon as you have a good idea about the nature of your attachment style, you can start working to eliminate the patterns that hinder growth. You are then – as a good self-leader in the making – ready to receive feedback, ask for help, extend your boundaries and dare to say 'no'. You are clear about your WHY, are disciplined in your HOW and consistent in your WHAT. You are now able to make optimal use of your filter and compass to express your dream. As a result, other people can hear you and can see clearly where you want to go. Some of them will even be willing to help you get there. By speaking your dream out loud, you also prompt others into action.

3.
THE POWER OF NON-VIOLENT (EMPATHIC) COMMUNICATION TO UNLOCK LOVE

As people we need words to understand each other and share things. This is a huge challenge. Communication is not about saying what you think. It is about making sure that the other can hear what you really mean.

Having some idea about how non-violent communication works can give you a push in the right direction. This is a way of communicating developed by the American psychologist Marshall B. Rosenberg, inspired by advocates of peace like Mahatma Gandhi and Martin Luther King. It is a dynamic communication model based on observation, feelings, needs and requests. The core of non-violence is found in the intention of the communicator not to harm the needs of others. To make this possible, there are three central and partially overlapping principles:
1) respect your truth force or love force *(satyagraha):* always follow the truth (as you see it);
2) never wound or harm *(ahimsa):* refrain from causing injury or damage to others;
3) be concerned for everyone's welfare *(sarvodaya):* take account of the needs of all interested parties.

By showing respect you increase the chance that you will be shown respect in return. Non-violent communication lowers the threshold for saying what is really bothering you. This allows you to express your dissatisfaction more positively, which is beneficial both for your own health and for your relations with others. It provides you with a way to channel anger and other emotions in a manner that promotes further discourse rather than breaking it off. As a result, the purpose of the discourse remains in focus at all times, even if emotions are involved.

If you want to know more, read the book *Vrede kun je leren* (Peace is something you can learn) by David Van Reybrouck and Thomas d'Ansembourg. The authors are convinced that peace education should be as much a self-evident part of people's upbringing as physical education and bodily care. According to them (but also backed up by the results of recent research), the teaching of techniques such as mindfulness, non-violent communication and compassion at school, at work and in the home will lead to higher self-esteem, better learning performance and greater mutual understanding. Or how sitting in silence for just ten minutes a day can improve the mental hygiene of both individuals and society as a whole.

'Peace requires something far more difficult than revenge or merely turning the other cheek; it requires empathizing with the fears and unmet needs that provide the impetus for people to attack each other. Being aware of these feelings and needs, people lose their desire to attack back because they can see the human ignorance leading to these attacks; instead, their goal becomes providing the empathic connection and education that will enable them to transcend their violence and engage in cooperative relationships.'
Marshall B. Rosenberg

Correct communication is important. It creates a climate favourable for speaking your dream out loud and for then pursuing that dream step by step, but always in connectedness with others. Let Love Rule...

Nadine Montens had already worked for a number of years in the coaching and training sector when she made a disturbing discovery. Even though the evaluation of her work was generally very positive, she began to realize that some of that work with some customers actually drained her of energy rather than increasing it.

Nadine: *'I became more and more aware that many of the people I was coaching felt themselves to be little more than a number. Even so, the feedback I received was good and new customers kept on coming to me for guidance. But for myself, I gained little satisfaction from what I was able to give them. I needed to find a different way to bring about an essential change that is at the core of my work.*

I went actively in search of my WHY and quickly came to the conclusion that it was not in the place I had previously thought. Or perhaps it had moved of its own accord? Be that as it may, from now on my priority was to give people back their self-esteem, to ensure that people who were regarded and treated as numbers would no longer see themselves in that same negative light. I wanted to restore their strength, so that they could tap the potential deep down inside them. I carried on giving my training, but instead of feeling tired and empty at the end of the day I now came home in the evening feeling full of beans! I believe strongly that if what you do is properly aligned with what you feel, this is a first and crucial intermediary step on the way to the realization of your dream. There is never an end point. No final destination. It is important to remain open for new opportunities. Your road is not fixed. I often feel like a ship at sea: time after time I love setting sail on the wide expanses of the ocean of freedom. But my journey is also a reasoned one. I don't let myself get carried away. In this context, I place great faith in signs. I believe we are here on earth to gain as much experience as we can. By observing and by following our own intuition, we move from station to station, from port to port. We must dare to say the things we want to say. But we must also dare to review those things critically. That is the only way to make progress. There is a saying in French that expresses it perfectly: La vie nous ressert toujours le même plat jusqu'à ce qu'on apprenne à le manger *(Life keeps serving us the same dish until we have learnt how to eat it). Only then are you ready for the next step, the following station, a new port. Give your full attention to everything that happens along the way. Because even though change begins on the inside, it is often triggered by things on the outside, in the world around you.*

By putting your dream into words, you construct your own inner foundations. These are vitally important. There are two types of foundations or pillars. The external ones (education, social norms, etc.) are those you build in collaboration with your environment. This means that you are also dependent on others to build them up again, if they ever get knocked down. As the name implies, the internal ones (talents, joy of life, etc.) are those you already have inside you, but you keep working on them your whole life long. Your inner pillars are the strongest. These are the ones you can always rely on. What's more, if, for whatever reason, they one day come crashing to the ground, you have the ability to rebuild them yourself.'

If you know yourself well, if you are a good self-leader, you will be capable of correct communication. This will make it possible for you to open yourself to whatever comes your way from the outside. Such honest accessibility brings us close to the discourse and the world of the artist. After all, what does an artist do? He waits, as it were, for external signs to activate his inner creative force and thereafter trusts that from this symbiosis of creative potential and momentum a work of art will be born...

Truth depends on the unexpected moment of change.

KOEN VANMECHELEN

‘It is during the STAND phase that creative fertility comes to full development. Something new and unexpected comes into being. What started as a dream now leads to the birth of a chicken – the chicken as a living work of art.’

nnection © KOEN VANMECHELEN, 2009

HOW TO PRACTICE 'STANDING UP AND SPEAKING OUT'

Whoever passes by decides
Whether I am tomb or treasure,
Whether I speak or remain silent.
You, and you alone, have this in your hands.
Friend, do not enter without desire.

PAUL VALÉRY *(1871-1945), poet, essayist and philosopher, on the pediment of the Palais de Chaillot in Paris*

How do you get stronger, strong enough to speak your dream out loud? Having a good understanding of your secure bases helps you grow towards self-leadership. The more self-leadership qualities you possess, the easier you will find it to mount the stage. And that is something that can also be learnt!

The following two exercises can help you speak your dream out loud.

1 identifying and strengthening your secure bases

Below you will find ten questions that can serve as an aid to make you better aware of your secure bases, the safe foundations that have helped you grow into the person you are today. This increased awareness will allow you to make further progress along the right path. You can do this exercise with someone who knows you well and with whom you feel safe. Let's call him/her your 'success watcher'. He/she asks the questions, you answer, and he/she writes down what you say.

1 Go back in your thoughts to your childhood and adolescent years. Who made you believe in yourself? Who encouraged you to make use of your potential?
2 Was the influence of one of these people ever decisive for you at a particular moment in time or for a particular event? We are looking here for a crucial turning point, something that still has an impact on your life today.
3 In what other ways have these people from your childhood and adolescent years had an influence on your life?
4 Have there also been people in your professional (adult) life who made you believe in yourself and encouraged you to make full use of your potential?
5 Think back to a moment when the influence of one of these people was decisive. What did they say or do?
6 Repeat questions 4 and 5, but this time look in your personal (adult) life.
7 As well as people, it is also possible for a goal, an idea, a dream or an event to stimulate us to get the best out of ourselves. Which goals, ideas, dreams or events have had a decisive influence at a crucial moment in your life?
8 Have you ever promoted self-esteem in others and encouraged them to make full use of their potential? What did you say or do? And how did the people concerned react?
9 Think back to a moment of failure, crisis or loss in your personal or professional life. Who did you turn to for advice? What did this person say or do that helped you further?
10 Was there ever a moment in your professional life when there was no one you could turn to for support and encouragement? If so, what effect did this have on you?

Having a good understanding of your secure bases helps you to grow towards self-leadership. The development of as many self-leadership qualities as possible is the best preparation for speaking your dream out loud.

2 strengthening your stage talents

As long as you keep your dream to yourself, it will be nothing more than a figment of your own imagination. It only becomes achievable when you speak it out loud in words. But that isn't always easy. So how can you do it? How can you mount the stage and shout out your dream, so that the world sits up and takes notice?

STEP 1

To begin with, you need to ask yourself what image the idea of 'speaking out your dream' conjures up in your mind. Is it something that instantly appeals to you? Do you say 'I can do that!'? Or do you say 'Can I do that?'?

If you hear yourself saying 'Yes, I can really do that!', think about who you want to tell your dream to. If you feel a little bit tense as a result, that is perfectly normal. Have you made your choice? Tell them your dream and move on to step 2.

If you don't have that 'Yes I can' feeling, try searching inside yourself to find whatever is stopping you from daring to speak out your dream. Perhaps you are afraid that you cannot clearly formulate what it is you want to say? Let people know where you are having difficulty. This will increase the chance that someone might be willing to help you. Practice speaking out your dream in front of a mirror. Better still, film yourself or ask someone else to do it. How does that feel? Do you think you can do it now? If you still feel uncertain, go back to the exercise in chapter 1 that asked you to search for your own unique talent, your identity. This is an ideal moment to make use of them! Try to find someone who makes you feel safe but isn't too close to you. Test out speaking your dream with him/her. Make clear that you don't find it easy, but do it anyway. You will be amazed at the magic this often creates...

If you find it hard to immediately start practicing with speaking out loud, you can try drawing or writing down your dream, or making a collage or a painting of it. This kind of preparation can help you find the words you want to use. Once again, you don't need to do this exercise on your own. Ask someone to help you. In the end, you will arrive at the right words. But be careful! If you end up with too many words, you will need to think again. To quote Simon Sinek: 'Great leaders talk about the future with such clarity that you would think they were talking about the past.'

STEP 2

You have now reached the point where you are ready to speak out your dream. Ask the person you have chosen to help you how it sounds. Don't ask him or her about the content – after all, it's your dream! But ask what message they picked up, what points they remembered. To confirm this, ask them to repeat the gist of what you have said. Don't forget: the purpose of communication is that others can hear and understand what you mean. Only then will they be able to support you in the realization of your dream. Let Love Rule...

Your secure bases have now become a transparent part of yourself. You have a clear view of their significance in your life. This makes you stronger. It gives you the strength to speak your dream out loud. You are now ready to mount the stage. So just do it – but don't be too disappointed if the first time doesn't work out as you had hoped. Like with everything in life, the golden rule for eventual success is practice, practice, practice!

Martin Luther King had a dream. But no matter how inspiring a dream may be, a dream that cannot come to life stays a dream. Dr King dreamed of many of the same things as countless other African Americans who grew up in the pre-civil rights South. He spoke of many of the same themes. He felt the same outrage perpetrated by an unjust system. But it was Dr King's unflappable optimism and his words that inspired a population.

SIMON SINEK, *from* Start with Why

PUSH,

The clearer the picture in one's Mind's Eye, the easier it will be to communicate it to others. This mental blueprint of what we want to build, this inner picture of something that has not yet happened, will ultimately guide the strategies that will make our visions a reality.

GEORGE KOHLRIESER, *from* Hostage at the Table

PUSH ON, PUSH YOUR DREAM INTO THE WORLD

YOU CAN SEE YOUR DREAM AND HAVE SPOKEN IT OUT LOUD. NOW IS THE TIME TO MAKE IT HAPPEN. DON'T GIVE UP. KEEP ON PUSHING, EVEN IF THINGS GET TOUGH.

You have visualized your dream. You have a clear picture of it inside your head. You have divulged it to the world. Whether you did this loudly or quietly does not really matter. The important thing is that the people around you now know who you are and what plans you are hatching. Every yes or no that you give in keeping with your inner self and your dream is a declaration of intent.

In this third phase – the phase that leads to the realization of your dream – the crucial thing is to be both consistent and persistent. But how do you do that? How can you live every day in harmony with your inner self? How can you keep on working at your painting?

To make this possible, you need discipline, perseverance and courage. Lots of courage. Courage to keep on believing in your dream. Courage to work at it step by step and day after day. Courage to find the mental strength to dredge up new reserves of enthusiasm whenever your spirits are low. Or in the words of Lenny Kravitz in his beautiful and oh so powerful song 'Push': *push the clouds away, push so you can see your way, push until you find your way home...*

WHEN I JOINED TOOLBOX IN 2008, two worlds opened up for me which I had never known before. Firstly, I was now operating in the non-profit sector (originally in Belgium, later globally), which is a world of good causes. The second new world was that of big money. Sometimes that money had been inherited from previous generations. Sometimes it had recently been earned by 'tech entrepreneurs'. I have always believed passionately in solidarity, but at the same time I realize that every euro invested in a philanthropic project has to be 'made' somewhere. For me, the logical follow-on of this is that every euro donated must be spent wisely and efficiently. It must make a difference. It must increase the impact of the good cause in a sustainable manner. That is not always as easy as it might sound. Those two worlds – the world of good causes and the world of big money – are separated from each other by a huge gulf. For this reason, I have a boundless respect for people who make it their mission to build bridges across that gulf. Perhaps you might not immediately think it, but this also takes courage and discipline, enthusiasm and perseverance.

I first met ***Alexandre Mars*** *almost in passing during my first early months as the chairwoman of ToolBox. During a meeting at the Rothschild Bank, the bank's director more or less produced him like a rabbit out of a magician's hat! 'I think it might be useful for you at ToolBox to meet the founder-chairman of the Epic Foundation.' I had never heard of the Epic Foundation and I had no idea who its chairman was. But following the director's brief introduction, the door opened and into the conference room walked a man oozing Gallic charm and accessibility, in a manner that for a few moments quite literally took my breath away. Once he began talking, he immediately moved me with his sincere interest in ToolBox and in the processes of donating for charitable purposes in Belgium. But it was his curiosity about our motives and drivers that finally convinced me that here was a man we could work with. I sat back and enjoyed the tornado of his personality sweeping through the room. It was clear to me that I was seeing and hearing a man at the height of his powers, confident in his own abilities and driven by his own passion to sustainably bridge the gulf in a field that was close to my heart. He had outlined the needs of both worlds with great precision. His words* *were well chosen and powerful: good causes must have systems and processes that work. Like any organization, they need good management (fortunately, the main focus of ToolBox!), so that philanthropists who donate money can be confident that it will not be wasted, but can have maximum impact.*

When I looked him up on Google later that evening, my already nascent admiration grew still further as I read through the story of his life. He was still only very young when his dislike of social injustice in combination with a remarkable talent for spotting up-and-coming trends planted the first seeds for what would later become Epic. By the tender age of 17, he had already started as a concert organizer and once he had completed his studies he quickly boarded the express train to commercial fame and fortune, setting up a succession of start-ups in digital marketing, mobile marketing and social network marketing. He quickly succeeded in putting each of these companies on the map and later sold them for sums that allowed him to amass considerable personal wealth. Alexandre Mars was just 39 when he sold his fourth start-up in 2013. He realized that he was now in a position to focus his attention on the objective that had really been his main long-term priority all along: building a world in which 'giving is the norm' (#MakeGivingtheNorm).

True to his origins as an entrepreneur, he carries out his own market research, which brings him into contact with philanthropic associations, experts in social development, postgraduates and researchers, the directors of non-governmental organizations, other social entrepreneurs, etc. Together, they seek to identify the problems for which solutions must urgently be found. It has become apparent that one of the biggest challenges is to repair the breach in trust between the donors and the non-profits. Equally important is the need to find new and creative ways to convince not only individuals but also major companies to adopt an attitude that will allow 'giving as a norm' to occupy a prominent place in their business models. Through the development of a series of transparent tools, the Epic Foundation has managed to establish itself in no time at all as a connective broker between on the one hand good causes with strong management and measurable, sustain-

able impact, and on the other hand potential benefactors who are prepared to participate in one of the many creative possibilities for making recurrent and systematic donations. For example, the monthly gifting of all the euro-cents after the decimal point on the pay slips of a company's entire workforce is just one example of the voluntary and painless options for putting this type of philanthropy firmly on the map – and into the collective conscience of the business world.

Every day since the setting up of the Epic Foundation in 2014, Alexandre Mars and his team have travelled the world, speaking from as many podia as they can in the hope of convincing their listeners of the sheer obviousness of giving. Right from the very beginning, 100% of all donations have been channelled to selected projects and good causes. And the operational costs? These are borne worldwide by its founder-chairman. Even so, he is still often the target of prejudice and condemnation. How genuine is his story? How sustainable are his solutions. 'It's easy to talk,' people sneer, 'when you've got as much money as he does!'

So what makes you want to keep on going in these circumstances?

LENNY KRAVITZ. Push

It's barely morning
Cars are roaring
The city's moving fast
My mamma's calling
But I'm stalling
Living in the past
It's time to face the world in front of me
And make the best of this reality

I'm going to push my life today
Push to make a better way
Going to push because I got to carry on

I'm going to push the clouds away
Push so I can see the way
Going to push until I find my way home

The jungle's swarming
Beasts are crawling
They're all along my path
But God's adoring, love is pouring
I'm going to take a bath
I am swimming in a violent sea
Trying to find out who I'm going to be

I can feel it come together
I know God has a plan, oh yeah
Oh, I see the kingdom through the shadows
But it's all gonna pass
I'm going to push
Because my Lord isn't going to let it last

I'm going to push until my Lord brings me home
Oh, oh yeah
Until I find my way home

1.
‘PUSHING’ YOUR OWN DREAM

Yes, I know. It would be nice, but sadly that’s not the way things work. Implementing the dream you have visualized and announced to the world seldom runs as smoothly as you would like. Between dream and deed there is a whole minefield of rules, regulations and practical objections. This is ‘the jungle swarming with beasts’ that Lenny Kravitz sings about. These obstacles mean that more often than not the road to your goal is anything but straight. Having said that – and this may sound a bit strange, perhaps blunt even – one of the biggest obstacles you will confront during your journey is... yourself. Doubts, fears, moments of disappointment, tiredness, a lack of conviction, fear of opposition, waiting for ‘more favourable circumstances’, the temptation to settle for something less than full success. These are just some of the possible factors that can cause you to lose sight of your dream, either temporarily or permanently. You may even turn your back on it altogether. But that would be a pity.

Whether or not you follow your dream to the end of the road will depend on how successfully you are able to activate three of the crucial anchor points in your growth.

Self-awareness

The more aware you are of your own needs and desires, the better you will be able to understand and accept your emotions – both the pleasant and the not-so-pleasant ones. And once you understand them, you can control them. Even so, it is by no means easy to push a dream into the world with success. You will encounter many different crossroads in your life, where choosing the right path depends on your ability to communicate in a connected manner. Again, this is where self-awareness can be a major help.

Self-control

Based on the conviction that all emotions necessary to reach your goal are acceptable, as long as they are expressed in an acceptable manner, you can fall back on your WHY to pull you through the difficult moments when you are overcome by tiredness, disappointment or sadness. It is at these moments, when you are on the point of throwing in the towel, that our specific human gifts – the gifts of self-awareness, imagination, conscience and free will – come to your rescue. They make it possible to respond to a provocative stimulus with the reaction of your choice from a wide range of different reactions. If you can do this with a good dollop of proactivity or self-responsibility – one of the core characteristics of self-leaders – you will be able to bring self-determinism and direction to your life. You only have a small degree of control over the things that will confront you on your journey to your dream. But that control can be multiplied each time you exercise your right of self-determination by offering a reaction in response to a stimulus. Or as Maya Angelou so stoically put it: 'You may not control all the events that happen to you, but you can decide not to be reduced by them.'

Self-motivation

Don't underestimate the power of enthusiasm in all this! An enthusiastic approach to your journey can make all the difference between reaching your dream – or not. Enthusiasm is infectious. It is often a decisive factor in determining the kind of life you lead and also has a huge impact on the lives of the people around you. It is like everything: too much of it is seldom good, but the right dose can work wonders. And the most wonderful thing of all? Enthusiasm is something you can grow!

The building up of self-awareness, the increase of self-control and the constant boosting of your self-motivation demand an active and positive attitude of non-stop effort and – perhaps most importantly of all – courage. Courage to strike the right balance between recklessness and cowardice. Courage to move forward one step at a time. Courage to get back up each time you fall. Courage to admit your failures and to accept the frustrations and disappointments of your journey without losing your way. Courage of the kind displayed so admirably in the life of Maya Angelou.

> COURAGE IS THE MOST IMPORTANT OF ALL VIRTUES, BECAUSE WITHOUT COURAGE YOU CAN'T PRACTICE ANY OTHER VIRTUE CONSISTENTLY. YOU CAN PRACTICE ANY VIRTUE ERRATICALLY, BUT NOTHING CONSISTENTLY WITHOUT COURAGE. **MAYA ANGELOU**

Maya Angelou – real name Marguerite Johnson – was an American writer and poet. Her life is the story of a black girl growing up in a racially segregated country and of a black woman who finally triumphed against the racism of the system. Notwithstanding the few months or years of relative security she experienced with her brother in the home of their grandmother, her youth was scarred by humiliation, neglect and sexual abuse, the latter inflicted by one of her mother's partners. At the age of fourteen, she listed her secure bases. They were: her grandmother and her determination; Mrs. Flowers (a prominent figure in the black community, who first gave Maya a sense that it was okay to be who she was, by offering her a job as a maid) and her books; Bailey and his brotherly love; her mother and her exuberant cheerfulness; Miss Kirwin (her inspirational teacher, who found her a place in an evening school for theatre and dance for both black and white adults); and her knowledge.

At the age of seventeen, Marguerite announced her intention to combine her schooling with training as a tram conductor – even though she learnt almost straight away that black people were never considered for this job. Nevertheless, her mother supported her in her wish, sending her on her way with the following frank but sound advice:

> THAT'S WHAT YOU WANT TO DO? THEN NOTHING BEATS A TRIAL BUT A FAILURE. GIVE IT EVERYTHING YOU'VE GOT. LIFE IS GOING TO GIVE YOU JUST WHAT YOU PUT INTO IT. PUT YOUR WHOLE HEART IN EVERYTHING YOU DO. AND PRAY. THEN YOU CAN WAIT. **MAYA ANGELOU'S MOTHER**

That was how Maya remembered her mother: as someone who always hoped for the best, was always prepared for the worst, and never let herself be surprised by anything that could happen in between. Notwithstanding the many hardships she suffered in her youth, the strength of this lesson in life remained with her.

When she was fifteen, Maya was wounded by her father's partner of the moment. She did not run away into the big, wide world, but waited patiently for someone to come and look after her. She was cared for by friends of her father, with whom she spent the night. This also shows that Maya was an icon of courage. Working at your dream also means accepting setbacks and facing up to the fact that things can sometimes go wrong. The secret is not to let it get you down. Just dust yourself off and take the next new step forward, and then another, with the same goal still fixed firmly in your sights.

> AT FIFTEEN, LIFE HAD TAUGHT ME THAT SURRENDER, SOMETIMES, WAS AS HONOURABLE AS RESISTANCE, ESPECIALLY IF ONE HAD NO CHOICE. **MAYA ANGELOU**

At the end of the 1950s, Maya worked as an actress in New York. There she became friends with many of the writers and artists who were active in the Civil Rights Movement. When the call of her African roots finally became too strong, she went via Egypt to Ghana. Her friendship with the human rights activist Malcolm X soon brought her back to the US, where they together set up a new human rights movement. In February 1965, Malcolm X was shot dead. Three years later, on April 4th, 1968 (Maya's 40th birthday), the leader of the Civil Rights Movement, Martin Luther King – the man who in 1963 had appealed for racial equality in his famous 'I have a dream' speech, given before a quarter of a million people in Washington D.C. – was also assassinated. Maya's grief at his death led her to publish the first volume of her controversial autobiography *I Know Why the Caged Bird Sings.* In a brave move for the time, she discussed the sexual abuse to which she had been subjected as a child. Many books followed and most of them were bestsellers. Later, she became friends with Oprah Winfrey, who repeatedly referred to Maya as one her most inspirational examples in life. The most important lesson that Oprah learnt from her was this: 'If you learn, teach. If you get, give'. At the inauguration of President Bill Clinton, Maya read at his request her poem *On the Pulse of Morning.* In 2013, in a US State Department video on behalf of the American people she declaimed her poem *His Day is Done,* a tribute to the life of Nelson Mandela. She died a year later.

OUTRAGE AT THE THINGS THAT ARE ACCEPTED AS THE STATUS QUO and therefore are supposedly beyond challenge; resistance to acquiescence in that status quo, based on the conviction that things can and must be different; the determination that drives someone to take the lead in the process of change: these are forces, if you have them inside you, that seldom sleep... We are back in my memories. In September 1989 – I will never forget it – the University of Ghent organized a study day on the theme of 'Women in Engineering'. As soon as it was announced, I registered to take part. I experienced an unbelievably inspirational day. But I also realized just how much work still needed to be done before women would be truly accepted in this male bastion. At the end of the day, a form was passed around asking if any of the women present – not men nota bene! – were interested in helping to set up a female engineering network. Notwithstanding this chauvinistic – one might even say misogynistic – introduction to the labour market, I didn't hesitate for a second. And so began what is still today one of the major chapters in my life story: my Vr&Ir adventure (Vr&Ir in Dutch stands for *Vrouw & Ingenieur* – woman and engineer). After the first meeting, I told my mother full of passion about the plans we had, the mountains we would move, the sacrifices we were prepared to make. But also about the doubts we had about setting up a 'women's only' network. Might this not simply perpetuate the divide between male and female engineers, rather than bringing them closer together? 'Do what you think you have to,' was her laconic answer. 'But remember that it will be a life's work.' As so often, she was right. Today, almost 30 years later, the network still exists – and is still as necessary as ever.

Each time I had doubts about the value and purpose of our female network, it was the words of a colleague-founder of a Dutch women's engineering network that put me back on track. When I first shared my doubts with her she answered: 'Do you know what, Hilde? Wherever we go as female engineers, we never have a mate we can meet and talk to in the toilet. That's not a problem men have got. So we've got to create our own place where we can meet our mates and talk to them – even in the toilet, if we want to!' She was right – and since then her words have helped me a lot. I realized – and still realize – that in the world of engineering female networks offer a safe place, a place that gives you strength, a place where you can find a little bit of extra courage when you need it. And as a woman in engineering you need a lot of courage to make your way, while still remaining true to your unique self. In this sense the mission of Vr&Ir is both empowering and altruistic. Its members are initially connected through their engineering studies, which form a common basis for a platform where people can grow in their different roles by experimenting, organizing and learning from each other.

Sounds easy? It wasn't. Right from the very start, it was painfully clear that it would cost blood, sweat and tears to convince people – including many women – of the justice of our cause. We organized events, trainings, debates and symposia galore, but the turnout was invariably low. There was plenty of applause from our small audiences, but this was seldom followed by mass registrations to join our ranks. Until a German colleague gave me a golden tip: 'If you expect ten people, only put out seven chairs, and not twelve.' What a difference in experience if all ten turn up, so that you need to go and get three extra chairs! Suddenly, we were playing to 'packed' houses – and the registrations began to come in.

It was also thanks to Vr&Ir that I learnt you should never be afraid to ask. Whether you are inviting a famous speaker, applying for subsidies or hoping to use a prestigious location free of change, remember that the worst that can happen is that people say 'no'. And who knows, perhaps they might say 'yes'!

Vr&Ir also made me sensitive to situations where women – just because they are women – are spoken to in a different way. Or where their actions are interpreted in a different way from their male colleagues. I have never been willing to let this pass. To give just one example. Whenever my only female colleague at ExxonMobil had to slip out of meetings early to pick up her kids from school, there were always comments like: 'I see she's leaving half way through again' – usually followed by laughter. One day when this happened, I pointed out to the men that it was strange that they encouraged me whenever I had to leave meetings early to follow my MBA course, whereas they poked fun at my colleague who had gone to keep an even more important appointment: with her own children. The next day, I explained to her the effect her manner of leaving the meeting had had. I suggested that next time – instead of just sneaking out of the room in silence – she should stand up proudly and declare: 'Lads, I'm just off to keep the most important appointment of my life!' She did – and there were no more comments after that.

The courage and the discipline you display to pursue your dream also make you capable of taking difficult decisions. What kind of decisions? Stopping with things that are not helping you move forward (even though you thought they would); not being afraid to change paradigm when things do not turn out the way you expected; above all, committing yourself without hesitation 200% to everything constructive that can assist you in reaching your goal. If you want to push your dream into the world, if you want to persevere with that dream when the going gets tough (as it will), it is essential for you to recognize that there is no single 'golden rule' that can tell you how to do this. It is up to you to find out whatever works best in your situation. How? By testing things, talking to others, seeking inspiration, reading books... Or to put it even more simply:
Begin!
Experiment!
Adjust!

> YOU ALONE ARE ENOUGH. YOU HAVE NOTHING TO PROVE TO ANYBODY. **MAYA ANGELOU**

The greater the insight you have into the specific talents that allow you to keep going or help you get back on your feet after a setback, the easier it will be for you to deal with the obstacles you will inevitably encounter on your way to realizing your dream. If your dream is strong enough, you will be able to weather even the severest storms. In spite of everything, you will get to the end of your road.

> I HAVE LEARNT THAT NO MATTER WHAT HAPPENS, OR HOW BAD IT SEEMS TODAY, LIFE DOES GO ON AND IT WILL BE BETTER TOMORROW. I'VE LEARNT THAT YOU CAN TELL A LOT ABOUT A PERSON BY THE WAY HE OR SHE HANDLES THESE THREE THINGS: A RAINY DAY, LOST LUGGAGE AND TANGLED CHRISTMAS TREE LIGHTS. **MAYA ANGELOU**

Remember also to take good care of yourself. There is only one person who is always with you – and that's you! Listen to your body, live in every fabric of your being, safeguard your mental hygiene. Keep in mind the four human dimensions according to Stephen Covey – the author of books like *The Seven Habits of Highly Effective People,* who has inspired more than 15 million readers worldwide:
Live! – the physical dimension
Love! – the emotional dimension
Learn! – the mental dimension
Leave a legacy! – the spiritual dimension

On a fine day in 1998, Alain Maus, the nephew of one of my colleagues at Kemira, walked into my office and into my life. When his training in the logistics department of the company came to an end, even though by that time he had obtained diplomas in both economics and marine science, the management initially thought he was too young to start in a more permanent and more responsible position. In contrast, I had recognized his potential from the very first day. Consequently, I let it be known that I was willing to take him under my wing and let him grow under my guidance. Ten years later, in Finland in 2008, Alain was one of the last survivors of the savage 'reorganization' I had been forced to implement. So far, I had helped every employee to find a new professional direction for the future. Now it was Alain's turn. For him, the moment had come for independence and entrepreneurship.

Alain: *'After ten years working abroad in a challenging environment where I had excellent relations with most of my colleagues and superiors, the huge clear-out at Kemira was a signal that triggered my intuition into action. It was time to turn my dream of becoming and independent entrepreneur into reality. The first two years were only semi-independent. I first gained further experience working as the communications officer for a tracking company. The big leap forward came when I designed a concept with one of the company's R&D people for a digital advertising board that could be changed automatically following the different times of day, different types of weather, different seasons, etc. At first, we had lots of difficulties to get permission to use the board at places we wanted. We ended up mounting it on trailers and using it wherever we could, including a handful of public buildings in our area. We didn't have the same network as the big players in the sector. As a result, things didn't take off in quite the spectacular way we had planned. Our income wasn't even sufficient to cover our costs. There was certainly no money over to pay us anything like a living wage. Even so, as soon as we were able to afford it we bought the building in which our office was housed and rented out the spare space to small start-ups.*

I was now the entrepreneur I had always dreamed of becoming. But it would still take years before I actually started earning any real money from it. My first step in the right direction was when I decided to participate in the venture of one of our lessees. This company had developed a machine for making ice cubes. In just a few years, we grew the company from a start-up with a single machine to a thriving business with seven machines. By now, we were delivering ice cubes in all different shapes and sizes to every corner of the country. In the early days, I still worked mornings in our original digital advertising office, neatly dressed in jacket and tie. But at lunchtime I pulled on my overalls and jumped happily into our delivery van to speed around Belgium with load after load of ice. It was a hectic life, but at the time I wasn't really bothered. I was having fun and I had helped to launch two small but modestly successful businesses, even though the economic climate was far from favourable. Many other companies were going under at this time. We were surviving – just.

I certainly gained great satisfaction from this 'successful' double leap into the freedom of entrepreneurship. But I was still looking for something else that would give us a bit more financial breathing space. I was fortunate that my wife had kept her steady job and had supported me to the hilt in both my business ventures to date. But for the future we wanted a little more security and stability. With this aim in mind, five years ago I set up a third company. I decide to move into yet another new area – this time in the growing market for fire detection and burglar alarms. Today, this is where I spend 90% of my time.'

In the conference room, there is just a single, simple frame hanging on the wall. It contains the following text:

> *START WHERE YOU ARE.*
> *USE WHAT YOU HAVE.*
> *DO WHAT YOU CAN.*
> *– Arthur Ashe –*

Contentment also hangs in the air. But something in Alain tells me that this interview is not yet over, that it is not yet time for me to leave. He wrinkles his forehead and wriggles uneasily in his chair. He still has something to say. I am silent and let him feel my space.

Alain: 'I now have three companies and I can allow myself a couple of long-haul holidays with my family each year. For the rest, I am not a particularly wealthy man. I don't live in a mansion and I don't have a flashy car. True, when I retire I can sell the office premises in which we are now sitting. But that's all. My biggest dream was always to earn money by exporting fresh ideas and to see a bit of the world while I was doing it. I wanted to experience the spirit of the first 18 years of my life, which I spent with my original family in various parts of Africa, followed by my years in Finland with Kemira. Over time, reality has taught me how to convert my big dream into a series of mini-dreams: for all four of us, our family holidays are the most wonderful and most carefree weeks of the year. Am I happy? In my private life, very happy.

In my professional life, perhaps I am more restless: I still keep on looking for new and better ideas. But take it from me: the balance I have found from having a stable relationship with my wife of more than 25 years and a great family with two wonderful and healthy kids gives me far more satisfaction than anything I could ever hope to experience in the business world.

Feeling good about who you are, communicating openly with the people around you, both at home and at work, so that there are no opportunities for misunderstandings to arise: these are the things that matter. The realization that I can achieve this day after day in both my private and professional environment gives me the feeling that I have been successful in life. If I had realized this earlier, I might have carried on working for someone else: fewer worries, shorter hours, more freedom. But I have no regrets. How did I manage to get through all the difficult times? A positive attitude, sharp intuition, good foundations and perhaps a little bit of luck: these were the things that helped me cope with all the risks and dangers of entrepreneurship. And while I was doing the things I knew I had to do, they also kept me on the path that leads to happiness.'

2.
OPENING YOUR DOOR TO HELP FROM OUTSIDE

To keep moving your dream forward demands non-stop effort and discipline. This in turn requires plenty of courage and enthusiasm, as well as a transparent insight into your inner self. Sounds difficult? It is. But there is good news as well. You are not alone! During this stage of your journey you will find that Let Love Rule is just around the corner and will keep on knocking at your door. And what will you find when you open that door? People from your environment, who know you well enough to have a significant impact on your ambition to push your dream into the world. People who are prepared to guide you, support you, share dangers with you, keep burdens and temptations away from you, and applaud you when you deserve it. But also to give you a kick up the backside when you deserve that as well. We can achieve nothing alone. We all need other people to walk with us along the path to our dream.

IF, LIKE ME, YOU HAVE IDENTIFIED 'inspiring people to rise above themselves' as your WHY, and if, like me, you are almost constantly using your unique talent for 'connecting people', you would be smart to open your door to a little outside help as quickly as you can! It is simple: the work that this involves is never finished. You can see new opportunities every day to further your life's work. For people like me, thinking up new dreams is a 24/7 activity. So is the arranging of parties and events. But what better way is there to create a fertile environment for bonding than bringing people together? All very true, of course, but it doesn't happen by itself. It takes organization. And not just organization. There is also pre-thought, during-thought and after-thought. Choices need to be made. Intermediary measures need to be taken. A script must be written – and followed. The list is endless. To ensure that everything runs smoothly, I need the help of someone else. That is the lesson that life has taught me.

The good thing about enthusiasm is that it can set all different kinds of powerful forces in motion. The problem with enthusiasm is that it sometimes lets you get ahead of yourself, so that you exceed certain crucial limits: the limits of your own (physical) possibilities; the limits of what your team is capable of doing at that particular moment; the limits of what others are able to give in terms of effort and commitment; perhaps even the limits of what you yourself are able to achieve within the time available. Because I know that enthusiasm is my most powerful motor, I need someone alongside me who knows where my brake is. Someone who points out that I am going too fast when I can't see it for myself. Someone who brings me back down to earth when I get carried away by my own euphoria. Let's just say that I won't get done what I need to get done without someone who sees it as his/her mission in life to act as my internal compass. Someone who can find their own WHY and HOW in the projects and tasks that occupy me day in, day out. Someone who taps me on the shoulder when the work load is too heavy and the task distribution out of synch. Someone who asks me critical questions: How do you think you can manage this? When are you going to get around to that? Where can you find the time to fit in next week's meeting? Can you keep that promise without reducing the quality you always insist on? Of course, letting someone into your life in this way can be a two-edged sword. It's not all moonshine and roses. The questions fired off at me are sometime highly confrontational. The comments I receive are not always easy to hear.

But that's what makes them so useful, crucial even. The person who can keep me on my toes has a mandate from me to do it – and I respect that mandate. Thank God I have been fortunate enough to find such a person on my travels through life. In fact, it is one of the most wonderful gifts that life has ever given me. It is the feedback, appreciation and criticism of this person who is so close to me that gives me the wings to fly; that helps me to push through when things are difficult; that makes sure I don't give up on my dream when the road to its realization seems longer than I thought. Together, we can search for new ways to reach that dream.

Together, we can discuss my doubts and fears. I know that she will always listen. I know that I can always ask her anything and get an honest answer. This is what people mean by 'love in action'. Or that, at least, is how I experience it.

The someone to whom I opened my door tumbled into my life in 1995 as my future Customer Service Representative at the moment when I had just changed jobs within ExxonMobil and had been appointed as Technical Sales Representative. She was ordering very chic planners – the Time Management brand – and suggested over the phone that she should order one for me.

Twenty years, twenty planners and lots of bonding later – in the meantime, our families and other personal circles of safety have also become intimately intertwined – I can no longer imagine my life without this someone in it. Or to use the words of Lenny Kravitz: 'Some people you meet for a season. Some people you meet for a reason.' Meet… **Miet!**

3.
HELPING TO PUSH OTHER PEOPLE'S DREAMS

What does the person to whom we open our door and whose help we accept, or perhaps have even actively sought, actually do? Or to put it slightly differently: what skills or talents – and therefore by extension what development tools – can you use to help someone push their dream into the world? The list is almost endless. What works for one dream will not necessarily work for another. What one person experiences as help is not always viewed as being helpful by someone else. The uniqueness of the helper is another important variable. Before we are no longer able to see the wood for the trees, it is probably a good idea if I give a list of the skills and tools that I use when I try to provide (professional) assistance for the realization of other people's dreams. The effectiveness of these skills and tools has been tried and tested, and therefore recognized as such. For the clear insight and powerful formulation of the list, I am grateful to the people whose names you will deservedly find in the word of thanks at the end of the book.

If you want to help push someone else's dream, you could do worse than to bear in mind (for example) the following seven action points: 1. show genuine interest in people; 2. make people think and think along with them; 3. empathize as much as you can with the other person's dream; 4. give unconditional support and generate enthusiasm; 5. teach the other person not to be blown off course by obstacles; 6. never hesitate to use your professional expertise; 7. use your network.

Show genuine interest in people

Everything starts with having genuine interest in people. What makes them tick? What are they good at? This interest will help you see through the roles that people play, so that you can find the real dream behind the (boastful?) facade. For example, someone might say that they want to work in sales, whereas what they really want is to travel more and not sit in an office from 9 to 5 every day. By showing genuine interest, you can bring people's real dreams to the surface.

Make people think and think along with them

Make people think about themselves, the world and their relationship with that world and with other people.

You can do this by repeatedly asking them questions. Use Simon Sinek's golden circle as a starting point and in particular the WHY question: 'Why do you do what you do?' The answer should help to explain and define everything the person does and doesn't do. But you also need to clearly know the answer to this question in your own case. You can only be authentic if you are fully aware of what drives you as person. Don't set yourself above others like some kind of expert. Instead, think along with them. Ask the right questions based on a disarming curiosity. Learn as much as you can: from the person concerned and from the wider environment in which you both operate (a colleague, a teacher, a CEO, etc.).

Empathize with the other person's dream as much as you can

People's visualized and spoken dreams are not all equally clear. Sometimes they are still looking for possible ways to give practical effect to something that they only sense as being their great dream. If you feel that someone's dream still needs to be worked out in more concrete terms, this is what you should do: listen actively, give the person space to talk about the dream, filter the information you receive, and test that you have understood correctly by summarizing what has been said and asking repeat questions. It helps if you are able to truly empathize with the dreams of others. If you can 'live the dream with them', as it were, you will be able to motivate them to dig deeper into the images in their mind, which will lead to clearer insights that can give the dream a more definite shape and form. In this way, you work as the co-designer of their dream.

A willingness to question your own paradigm is essential for the successful use of this tool.

Give unconditional support and generate enthusiasm

Give empowerment real substance. Many leaders claim to give responsibility to their team members, but in reality keep effective power in their own hands, correcting what they see as 'errors' whenever they feel it is necessary. To really help people push their dreams into the world, it is important when delegating responsibilities to fully support the choices and decisions they make. Let the world see that you trust them! Let the world see that you think they are right! This unconditional support is important in giving them the courage to take the sometimes difficult steps that are necessary to reach a goal or an ambition – or even a dream! Away from the professional sphere, this process can be more generally described as 'generating enthusiasm'.

Try convincingly to take away the doubts that people often have when they finally need to take the practical steps that can lead to the realization of their dream. Encourage them as much as you can to stretch their own boundaries and inspire them to reach further than they have ever reached before.

Teach the other person not to be blown off course by obstacles

Demonstrating a positive attitude and an optimistic approach to life has a motivating and inspirational effect. In that way, you give concrete substance to your conviction that everything is possible, even if there are obstacles along the way. In this way, you create an atmosphere of 'We [and by extension, "you"] can do this!' It is best to approach problems with a similarly buoyant attitude: 'We can solve this!' Adopting this kind of positive but realistic frame of mind – you don't ignore or deny that the problems exist – gives lots of energy. As a result, it helps, supports and motivates the other person to implement his/her dream. Hope is a powerful motor to bring the best out of someone.

Never hesitate to use your professional expertise

Offering professional advice and assistance can also help people to realize their potential. This might include self-reflection questionnaires, inspiring stories, shared experiences with other participants in a professional group trajectory (known at TRAJECTUM as TRAJECTWAY), feedback from others, personality tests that can help to gain deeper insights into a person's inner self, etc. Even something as simple as finding a quiet space and thinking hard about what you want (and why) can have a positive effect. During coaching sessions, offering concrete tips can also have a powerful impact. Sometimes the gulf between dream and reality is so wide that you need to encourage the person to start by taking small steps towards their goal. Perhaps they could drop in for a coffee with the person who has the job, passion, etc. that they also dream of one day having. Or maybe they could test out their dream in the context of voluntary work. This will give them a more realistic impression of how far they still have to go.

Use your network

A well-maintained network is worth its weight in gold. When, for whatever reason, you are not able to provide the help your dreamer needs, calling in a 'specialist' from your network can work wonders. This allows you to deal effectively with unforeseen circumstances but also to compensate for any gaps in your own expertise. Most importantly, it means that there is always someone available to offer support and assistance when it is most urgently required.

In short, broaden people's horizons, stimulate change and show that reality really can be bent to our will. Act in the spirit of Edison, who once said: 'I have not failed a thousand times. I have successfully discovered a thousand ways NOT to make a light bulb.'

What I will always remember about Gerard Mortier was his infectious and irrepressible energy – always with a purpose, but at the same time also open for anything that came across his path. This is the true power of greatness. Mortier was one of those people who I like to describe as 'stoves': they radiate heat, they warm your heart, and when you are near them you feel a remarkable kind of energy that instantly lights up your whole being.

When Mortier talked about resistance to his vision, opposition to his approach, you could see his eyes sparkle with delight – a truly wonderful experience. 'Friction gives warmth,' he once said. I can think of no better remark to characterize the man he was.

STEFAN HERTMANS, *author and poet in* De Standaard *newspaper*

Every organism needs another organism to survive.

KOEN VANMECHELEN

‘PUSH, for me, is the stiffening of life, the fixing of momentum – the stuffed chicken. Remaining upright, keeping your head above water in spite of the pressure: that can hurt. It is urgency that you can see at work here.’

and Mortality – C.C.P © KOEN VANMECHELEN, 2014, PHOTO PHILIPPE VAN GELOOVEN

HOW TO PRACTICE 'PUSHING AND PERSEVERANCE'

How shock-absorbent are you?
How good is your suspension
if you have to pass over
the bumps of life?

The bumps and potholes
and stones along the way.
On highways and byways.
On motorways perhaps least.

But there you have that rushing,
speeding past
everything that is beautiful.

Give me the lumps and bumps of
the country road.
If you travel slowly enough,
the shocks are really not
that bad.

GEERT DE KOCKERE, *'maker of literary caprioles'*

Many different things are necessary to help people persevere when the realization of their dream proves more difficult than they thought. Circumstances, the personalities of those involved, opportunities, resilience, endurance, coping strategies, attitude, emotional intelligence, baggage and context, mental space: these are just some of the many relevant factors. Is it then a futile gesture to try and increase someone's store of courage, enthusiasm and persistence? Or to increase the likelihood that the arrows someone fires hit the target? Of course not! Every change process – like every journey – begins with a single step. And every step you take to do something in your life better or differently brings you closer to your final destination.

Approaching someone you think can help you to realize your dream takes courage. But it also takes courage from the helper – the 'courage-giver', if you like – to offer the tips and advice expected from him/her. Once you have gathered together this courage and are ready to act, it is in everyone's interests that your good intentions have the right impact. There is one golden tip that can help you to maximize your message's chances of success: always be present in the moment and always listen carefully to what others say. It is only by having a clear understanding of the impact of your words that you will be able to move closer to your common goal.

> An insight that can help to encourage **perseverance:**
> always be present in the moment!

Make time to talk to people properly. We humans find it difficult to do lots of things at the same time. During a conversation, it is important that you are present in the moment with your whole body and mind, so that you can pick up signals from your conversation partner. Be aware that during a conversation the biggest impact (56%) is created by your body language. 37% is created by the intonation of your voice. Just 7% is created by what you actually say. In other words, not very much.

> Another insight that can help to encourage **perseverance:**
> make yourself open for what you are going to hear!

Prepare the conversation thoroughly. Make time and room in your head and your heart, so that in the first instance you can listen properly to yourself. To begin with, don't mention the solution or the answer you would like to hear. Just say what you need, not how you expect it to be provided.

Don't judge. Listen to the other person with compassion. Show empathy, but do not lose yourself in the other's story. Whoever speaks or listens with compassion is less quick to feel attacked or criticized by their conversation partner's reactions (or lack of them). Ignore the patterns you already have inside your head. Also ignore any labels you might have stuck on to the other person in the past. Do not see an initial conflict of opinions as a barrier, but as an opportunity.

> The golden tip for maximizing **perseverance:** whoever takes good care of themselves has more courage and a better chance of persevering with success.

Creating space for yourself is essential if you want to cope successfully with the ups and downs of life. And it is the same with the path leading to your dream. Don't make the mistake of thinking this path will be easy. At times, it will be hard. Very hard. And if you are already at the limits of your strength and endurance when the problems arise, you won't be able to make the extra effort necessary to keep you on track. Making space for yourself is something individual. You know best what gives you energy, what can boost your enthusiasm. Make sure you save room for these things in your day, your week, your month. Perhaps you need a little time to plan something more solid that can prevent you from being steamrollered by the (often self-imposed) obligations and (seeming) inevitabilities of life. However, there is nothing to stop you from seeking some instant energy by immediately adding a little bit of 'white space' to your daily routine. Making 15 minutes' time for yourself each day is an incredibly worthwhile and rewarding habit. Silence around you and silence in your head brings you back into contact with yourself.

At the start, 15 minutes might seem too long. If so, start with five minutes and gradually increase the duration. You will be amazed just how refreshing and inspirational this can be. It is guaranteed to increase the quality of your life. You will feel that you have more control of things and of yourself. You can do it either at the beginning or end of your day. Which suits you the best? The only way to find out is to try it and see!

'Bod Pa!'
'Yeeees!'
Peregrin increases his pace to catch up with him. 'Now we can have some fun. But what happens if heaven falls on us?'
'What a question, Peregrin! Then we will carry heaven on our shoulders and keep on walking.'
'But we are doing that already. And you are letting me carry the heaviest bit.'
'Okay, so let's swap places. Can we carry on now?'
'Yes, we can carry on.'

ANTON QUINTANA *(1937-2017), author, in 'The Book of Bod Pa'*

LET LOVE RULE

Try to be the rainbow in someone's cloud.

MAYA ANGELOU

LET LOVE RULE FOR THE REALIZATION OF YOUR DREAM

WHETHER YOU ARE TRYING TO REALIZE YOUR OWN DREAM OR ARE HELPING SOMEONE ELSE TO REALIZE THEIRS, AND IRRESEPCTIVE OF YOUR OTHER MOTIVES AND DRIVERS, THERE IS ONE FUNDAMENTAL PRINCIPLE YOU MUST ALWAYS RESPECT:

LET LOVE RULE!

The motor that keeps things turning in this world of ours is nothing less than… the power of love. A cliché as tall as the Empire State Building? Maybe. But that doesn't stop it from being true, does it? *Amor vincit omnia:* love conquers all. Surely we would all agree with that, wouldn't we? Mmmm. Sadly, it is all too easy to find examples of what can happen when love very clearly fails to 'conquer all', when it is replaced by something less wholesome. Might it be that we understand the amazing potential of love, but that in practice we are somehow unable to automatically make use of this potential in the things we do? Pride, powerlessness, anger, shame… there are so many obstacles that can stand in the way of love. So let's complete the circle and end our story by asking out loud – and then explaining – exactly how love can make the difference. In everything. Even in our process of dream realization, whether in terms of actually being a self-leader or in terms of cherishing and protecting those who are on their way to becoming one. To penetrate deeply into the hearts and minds of those who are still in doubt. In the hope that the early adopters in all our environments will stand up and be counted, offering the last bits and pieces of help that will enable the final transformation. But before we start, let's once again call on influencer Lenny Kravitz to show us the way.

LENNY KRAVITZ. Let Love Rule

Love is gentle as a rose
And love can conquer any war
It's time to take a stand
Brothers and sisters join hands

We got to let love rule
(Let love rule)
We got to let love rule
(Let love rule)

Love transcends all space and time
And love can make a little child smile
Oh can't you see
This won't go wrong
But we got to be strong
We can't do it alone

We got to let love rule
(Let love rule)
We got to let love rule
(Let love rule)

You got to got to got to
(Let love...)

1.
LOVE FROM AN UNEXPECTED QUARTER

The fact that help and support – love! – can sometimes come from where you least expect it is one of the key messages I want to give through this book. However, this help and support – this love! – can only do its 'work' if the receiver is willing to accept it. For that reason, it is vitally important that you consciously and actively open your mind to things that you perhaps do not yet understand, to things that you never expected, never mind that you would one day be able to rely on them. Once this message has sunk in, you are ready to accept and honour the invitation to go on a fascinating voyage of discovery. Go exploring. Approach people who you perhaps first thought were not so approachable, people you would never have chosen to do so in the past. Dare to make space in yourself for the things that are different in others. Be confident that this will have an inspirational effect, allowing you to reach and make contact with different places, different habits, and different ways of relating to life. If you have watched, weighed and dismissed something, take a deep breath and, out of respect, have a look at it a second time. Respect (from the Latin *respicere,* meaning 'to look at' or 'to take account of') is something you show through your behaviour and has its origin in a conviction, a decision of the mind. It is a 'yes' to others. Not a 'yes' as a response to someone else's demands, but a 'yes' to everyone's fundamental humanity. Go into the world without judgement and allow yourself to be surprised, but remember also that sometimes things will not work out. Even so, it will always have been worth the effort of having tried. Fortunately, there is always an exit. Just press ctr + alt + del and forget about it. In all other cases, what you can gain is pure profit.

A remarkable figure who has dedicated his life (and still does) to the preservation of peace – in the sense of helping to maintain the power of love throughout the world – is William Ury, a man with his own unique and remarkable view about what we mean by the 'unexpected quarter'.

William Ury studied anthropology, linguistics and classical languages. He was co-founder of the Harvard Negotiation Program and a consultant for the American Government and a number of large multinational companies. Ury was also active as a conflict mediator in the Middle East, the Balkans, the former Soviet Union, Indonesia, Chechnya and Venezuela. Together with Roger Fisher, he was the co-author of a handbook for international negotiators: *Getting to Yes: Negotiating Agreement Without Giving In,* which first appeared in 1981, followed by a second edition in 1991 (now with Bruce Patton as co-author) and a third edition in 2012. The book has sold five million copies in more than twenty languages. 2015 saw the publication of *Getting to Yes with Yourself and Other Worthy Opponents,* in which Ury underlines the importance of knowing what you need to make the most of your potential. This, he argued, keeps you closer to who you really are, so that you have your feet more firmly planted on the ground. For me, this conviction, in combination with respect as a basic attitude in your dealings with others, is 250% Let Love Rule. From *Getting to Yes,* where the focus was on 'the other' and how you can win them over to your side, in *Getting to Yes with Yourself* Ury arrives at the insight that everything begins, as the title suggests, with yourself. His approach makes use of concepts like 'the third side' and 'the balcony perspective' to develop solutions for conflicts. What we need to do, according to Ury, is take a step back and view obstacles at a distance. In this way, we can see them in a new light and find an 'eighteenth camel' that will bring the situation to a successful conclusion.

> A MAN HAD SEVENTEEN CAMELS.
>
> WHEN HE KNEW THAT HE WAS DYING, HE CALLED HIS THREE SONS TO HIM TO SHARE OUT HIS PROPERTY BETWEEN THEM.
>
> TO HIS OLDEST SON HE LEFT HALF OF HIS CAMELS.
> TO HIS SECOND SON HE LEFT A THIRD OF HIS CAMELS.
> TO HIS YOUNGEST SON HE LEFT A NINTH OF HIS CAMELS.

WHEN THE OLD MAN DIED, THE SONS CAME TOGETHER TO CLAIM THEIR INHERITANCE. BUT THEY SOON FOUND THEY HAD A PROBLEM: SEVENTEEN IS NOT DIVISIBLE BY TWO, THREE OR NINE!

THEY BEGAN TO DISCUSS HOW THEY COULD SOLVE THIS PROBLEM, BUT SOON ENDED UP ARGUING. NO MATTER HOW HARD THEY TRIED, THEY COULD NOT SEE A SOLUTION. IN DESPERATION, THEY WENT TO SEEK ADVICE FROM A WISE OLD WOMAN.

SHE THOUGHT FOR A WHILE AND THEN SAID: "I DON'T KNOW WHETHER IT WILL HELP YOU, BUT I ALSO HAVE A CAMEL I NO LONGER NEED. PERHAPS YOU WOULD LIKE IT?"

THE THREE SONS NOW HAD A TOTAL OF EIGHTEEN CAMELS.
THE ELDEST SON TOOK HIS HALF – HALF OF EIGHTEEN IS NINE.
THE SECOND SON TOOK HIS THIRD – A THIRD OF EIGHTEEN IS SIX.
THE YOUNGEST SON TOOK HIS NINTH – A NINTH OF EIGHTEEN IS TWO.

THEY HAD NOW EACH TAKEN THEIR SHARE AND HAD DISPOSED OF SEVENTEEN CAMELS: NINE PLUS SIX PLUS TWO. BUT THERE WAS STILL ONE CAMEL OVER. "WHAT SHALL WE DO WITH THIS ONE?"

THEY GAVE IT BACK TO THE WISE OLD WOMAN...

A TRADITIONAL MIDDLE EASTERN TALE, OFTEN TOLD WITH PLEASURE BY **WILLIAM URY**

In 2007, Ury launched his Abraham route initiative, a walking route that follows in the footsteps of the biblical Abraham, from his original birthplace in the city of Urfa in southern Turkey to his burial place in Hebron. This means that the route passes through the heart of the zone of conflict in the Middle East. It is a wonderful non-profit, non-religious and apolitical initiative that seeks to create connections of many different kinds (ecological, touristic, sociological, cultural, etc.) between this troubled region and the rest of the world. In April 2014, the British *National Geographic Traveller* chose the Abraham route as No.1 in its list of the ten best-ever walking routes on the planet. In addition, it is also an unparalleled Let Love Rule vehicle, where each day incredible bonding takes place and fantastic stories are created. In a part of the world where fear of the strange and hostile 'other' dominates, the Abraham route surrounds the people who walk it with love.

'THINK OVER THE WEEKEND IF YOU CAN WORK WITH STUPID PEOPLE.' Seldom had I been approached in such explicit terms about my willingness to leave behind my own tribe and throw in my lot with new and unknown tribes, hoping that I would be accepted by them like in my tribe of origin. I had survived all the preliminary rounds. I had passed all the tests with flying colors. I could hardly wait to make the step from the oil mega-giant ExxonMobil to the small Finnish chemical dwarf Kemira. I would lead a Purchasing and Logistics Team, but above all I was looking forward to see how my interest in the way people are put together – which over the years had superseded my interest in the way things are put together – would work out in practice. For many years, I had operated in an environment where everyone shared the same identical orientation, with ambition, intelligence, passion and determination as the common characteristics. We all had only one thing in our sights: to move forward as far and as quickly as we could, both for ourselves and the company. But in my new place of work I would find myself in a very different biotope. As 'leader' of the Purchasing and Logistics Team, I would need to learn to work with people of many different types in terms of their commitment and motivation.

Although I had already said 'yes' – I could hardly wait to start – a final obstacle was now placed in my way in the shape of the question that I was asked. Could I really work with stupid people? I thought about it and stuck with my original decision. The future would show whether I was right or not. I was a leader who stood among her people (mostly men), who trusted them (and made that clear), who listened to them (and then built further on the information I received). And if the men still had doubts, we looked together under the machines and got our hands dirty. We searched in partnership for a solution. I now know that during those years I was not guided exclusively by my willingness to leave my tribe. It was the love for people that saved me. In every situation, time and again. And it still does.

Being prepared to explore, being prepared to tread unfamiliar pathways to reach what you can see at the top of the mountain, even though you have no clear idea how you are going to get there: this is without doubt one of the best ways to work actively towards the achievement of your dream. Safe in the knowledge that love, help and support sometimes come from unexpected quarters, it is important to start your journey free from all preconceptions and prejudices. This is something that William Ury so beautifully illustrates in his stories through his repeated reference to the following fragment of poetry:

> HE DREW A CIRCLE THAT SHUT ME OUT –
> HERETIC, REBEL, A THING TO FLOUT.
> BUT LOVE AND I HAD THE WIT TO WIN:
> WE DREW A CIRCLE AND TOOK HIM IN.
>
> A FRAGMENT FROM *OUTWITTED*
> BY THE POET EDWIN MARKAM (1852-1940),
> FREQUENTLY QUOTED AS AN ILLUSTRATION
> OF HIS OWN CONCEPT OF 'RESPECT' BY
> **WILLIAM URY**

Or how exclusion can be transformed into inclusion. And how that can bring you closer to the realization of your dream.

On a larger scale – with world peace as the collective dream of mankind – this same rhetoric has been professed by more than one leader with far-reaching impact. In a powerful TED talk that he gave directly from the Vatican in April 2017, Pope Francis explained why the only future worth building is a future that includes everyone. He ended with the words: 'Tenderness is the path of choice for the strongest, most courageous men and women. Tenderness is not weakness; it is fortitude. The future is, most of all, in the hands of those people who recognize the other as a "you" and themselves as part of an "us". We all need each other.' And in two newsletters in January 2018, Matthieu Ricard, best known as the personal translator of the fourteenth Dalai Lama and author of books on Buddhism and Eastern philosophy, appealed to his readers in much the same way. Based on his conviction that altruism alone can save mankind and the planet, he summarized the philosophy of the book *Ensemble* by Sébastien Henry, for which Ricard wrote the foreword, with as much passion as the original author: 'All life forms depend for their continued existence on each other and their environment. Mankind does not escape from this need to live together. Imagining that each of us is an isolated unit, capable of creating our own happiness within our own egocentric soap bubble, is by nature dysfunctional and can only lead to permanent dissatisfaction. Our joys and our pains only exist in relation to and through the intercession of others. Would love serve any purpose if we each were to hang in space like a piece of string? Our understanding of this mutual dependence must be reflected in our desires, our engagement and our manner of being.'

If every person on earth were to stretch out his or her hand to another person... If, by so doing, every person on earth received love from the other person in return, perhaps even from an 'unexpected quarter'...

'You grew up in a dysfunctional family: in the stranglehold of alcoholism and violence. It is no coincidence, it seems to me, that your statues are made from bits of junk and debris. Are you trying to put the pieces of your life back together?'

(emotional) 'God, who knows. Perhaps my work is just a giant repair job. I started making my statues when I was fifteen. I wanted to have something to touch, something indestructible to hold on to. A teacher gave me the push I needed. He showed me things that I had never known before: respect, warmth, affection. He was even careful with materials. I can still remember vividly how amazed I was when I saw him mould a lump of clay with such tenderness into a sculpture. I was sold instantly. I still am. That teacher not only tapped into my talent; he also laid a hand on my shoulder. I was okay, I belonged. And what I was doing was okay as well. I was off and running. With some clay and other bibs and bobs I began making figures that did what my parents failed to do: protect me.'

JOHAN TAHON, *sculptor, in an interview with Jelle Van Riet in* De Standaard *newspaper*

2.
LOVE 'FROM WHERE YOU CAN EXPECT IT'

Your self-chosen partner for life, the children from that relationship, brothers and sisters, cousins, nieces and nephews, parents and parents-in-law, friends... these are all people who you would expect to show you love. Just as you would expect to show them love in return. Surely that is self-evident, part of the natural order of things? This expectation is usually justified and your loved ones respond in a correct and concrete manner. The potential for love that can be exchanged through these channels has an immense power. But when this love 'from where you can expect it' is lacking, this can often clip the wings of people flying toward their dream. And more often than not it is difficult to get those wings going again.

Sometimes the love 'from where you can expect it' falls away as a result of forces beyond the control of those involved. All you can then do is wait and pray that you will be able to find something to replace what has been lost.

It was a freezing cold winter's night with treacherous icy roads when Annie Swennen, who had just given birth to her third child and was still recovering in the maternity unit of her local hospital, received the news that her husband, who was a general practitioner, had been killed in a car accident. While he was on his way to visit a patient, his car had skidded off a bridge just a few kilometres from their home. Luc Reyntens was 32 years old. Annie was 29. The tragedy is still a fault line in her life...

Annie: *'Talking about the disaster that overwhelmed me that day is still difficult, even 40 years later. It was 21 January 1978. Our oldest children were three-and-a-half and two years old. Our youngest son less than a week... Luc was 23 when we first met. He was in his fourth year studying medicine. At the time of the accident, we had been married for four years. We were just on the point of buying a plot of land to build a house where he could have* *his doctor's surgery as well. We were a good team. I did the administration and the telephone for Luc, gave some first basic information to the patients and also offered them a listening ear when it was needed. Even though his practice was getting busier all the time, we were very happily married and had already started to build a loving family. The future seemed to be smiling on us. It was a fairy tale, a dream, almost too good to be true...*

And then came that awful blow. In a single terrible moment I lost my husband, my best friend, the father of my children, my home – at the time we were living in a rented house with a surgery – and all my dreams. The pain was immense. I could still feel it physically, for months, even years afterwards. People thought that they had to try and cheer me up, said that I should be strong for the children, that I would pull through. Whereas for a long, long time all I wanted was to be alone with my pain. Alone and with my children. My parents were the only ones who gave me a bit of space. They never told me what I was supposed to think, do or feel. My dad took over a lot of the domestic things. He came to work in the garden, do odd jobs around the house, and goodness knows what else. He was always there for the kids and they gave him so much love in return. I could also count on the support of a handful of others: my sister, with whom me and the kids did various city trips, and my mother, with whom I have always had a special bond...

In this way, I learnt to understand the importance of being 'encircled', of 'being there for somebody', of 'letting someone know you are thinking of them', but without further directives or advice, no matter how well-intentioned. Like my dad said to me so often: 'Annie, you need to keep hold of the strings that connect you to people and to life.' Which is precisely what I said to him a few years ago, as he gradually began to slip away, hoping I could now give him something to hold on to in the last conscious days of his life. I followed his advice. I kept hold of the strings, also with my friends and colleagues. Perhaps most special of all, also with my in-laws. Each year around January 21st both families still come together for a glass of champagne and a chat.

During the early years after the accident I sometimes consulted a child psychiatrist. I was uncertain whether or not I was giving the children what they needed. From her I learnt that as long as I kept moving forward, however slowly, they would be able to move with me as well. So no matter how difficult it was, I kept on doing all the things that parents do – tucking them up in bed, reading them a story, playing with them – because I felt it was important. And do you know what? Since then, I have never stopped surrounding myself with people and children.

In the meantime, my children have now grown into three wonderful, strong and caring people. As for me, I was fortunate enough to have a fascinating 35-year career as a teacher of Latin, French and history at a local school, where my colleagues and the pupils also helped enormously to carry me further through life. Now that I am retired, I look after my grandchildren a few times a week and I still give extra out-of-school lessons at home. I cannot image my life without children, who I embrace with warmth and love. Where I can, I want to try and be there for others, sharing with them some of the great love that has always remained within me. A store of love that has been constantly topped up over the years by my children and grandchildren, by all the children I have ever taught, and by all the sweet, kind people around me. So much love, so much warmth, so many friendly pats on the shoulder… You wouldn't believe how much strength this has given me, so that after all these years, and never forgetting the terrible loss I have suffered, it finally gives me peace of mind to say that I haven't done so bad. And it has certainly made me more receptive and sympathetic to the loss and sadness of others.'

On the obituary card for Luc's funeral, Annie and her family had printed a verse from the Bible: 'I shall be with you always, even to the end of time'. (St. Matthew. 28.20). They added two further sayings by Rabindranath Tagore: 'Let your love stay with me, even through the barrier nearness' and 'My last greeting is to those who gave me their trust, who were my friends and who loved me.' I can see that the nearness still lives for Annie, every day. Just as I am on the point of telling her this, she suddenly stands up and goes into an adjoining room. She returns with a recent edition of Paris-Match. *'There's an article in it about Alain Delon, who is now 82 years old. People used to tell me that Luc looked a bit like Alain Delon, with his dark hair and his deep blue eyes. I went and bought a copy because I was curious to see what my Luc might look like now, if he were still alive today…'*

And then the doorbell rings. Our conversation comes to an abrupt end. A pupil stands on the doorstep, waiting to come in. Annie thought that she had cancelled the lesson for today… But once a teacher always a teacher. I can see the old instincts coursing through her veins. And I can sense the love, too. I leave her to it.

Love 'from where you might expect it' may seem self-evident, but it can take as many different forms as there are people to give it. One instance of brotherly love is never exactly the same as another. The support you get from your parents can also vary enormously. So too does the help you receive from family, friends and your partner. But there is one thing they must all have in common – or that, at least, is what I think. If they really want to help you to unlock your talents and realize your dream, they must dare to be critical. *'Donde hay confianza, da asco',* as the Spanish say. Which loosely translated means: 'If the bond is strong enough, there is no need to wear masks.' In other words, when you are dealing with people who love you, there is no need to dissemble. When people already know you through and through, there is no point in attempting to hide the less pleasing aspects of your character and behaviour beneath 'the cloak of love'. Do we always like hearing these things? Of course not. Would we prefer to be praised as often as possible and criticized as little as possible? Another no-brainer. But that doesn't help you to move forward in life. The love of others only has meaning if it can speak freely.

I HAD BEEN WAITING FOR HER FOR YEARS. I already had a brother, but he was only two years younger than me and I so wanted a baby doll to play with! I was in the first year at primary school by the time this moment finally arrived. I could hardly contain my excitement, running around our village and blurting out the good news to anyone who would listen. I had already imagined it so often and there had been several false alarms. But this time it was true! My mother was pregnant!

On the day when the birth was expected, we had to go on a school trip. All that day I never let go of Miss Maria's hand. I wasn't going to risk falling off one of the swings or roundabouts in the playground. I wanted to make sure I would be back on time in Wezemaal to greet the arrival of my new sister. I came through the day safely and made it home in one piece. But even then my patience was still put further to the test. When we entered my mother's room during visitor's hour we found her there alone. The baby needed some extra care and had been taken back to the operating theatre! By the time I was finally allowed to see her the next day, she was behind the glass of an incubator, with her little legs bound together and wires and tubes sticking out of her. I understood that it might still take a little while longer before I could hold her and play with her. Even so, there she lay, my baby doll! Her name was **Griet.** And I wasn't even allowed to touch her!

When the cares and worries of the early months were behind us at last, we began our life 'together'. My brother Geert and I played in the sandpit, while little Griet played along in her playpen. As soon as she could speak, Griet became 'all mine'. She spent hours sitting next to me, playing school in our 'class'. By the time she was three, she could already read and do sums. I put her on the back of my bike and together we rode to school. We played in the garden or in our doll's house in the cellar, imitating the world we saw around us. I was the school teacher and the shopkeeper; Griet was the pupil and the customer. If, as often happened, Geert and some of the other kids from the street joined us, we played 'house'. Griet and the boy next door pretended they were a couple; so did Geert and the girl next door. I was 'mother', the one who kept everything together.

Griet grew up and started her own life. I was still there, at a distance, and kept a watchful eye to make sure that everything was alright with her.

A friend who came to our home to give me extra lessons in mechanics played with Geert and Griet, while I struggled to complete his exercises. Later on, I got to know Griet's friends as well. The door was always open in our house and people were forever coming and going. When Griet went off to study in Leuven, I decided to do an MBA and brush up on my languages. In the evenings I went along to her student digs and passed the time with her and her fellow students. In that way, our lives remained closely intertwined.

Griet was still young when I went through a number of difficult periods in my life. Although she didn't fully understand what was going on – I didn't really understand it myself – she was always there for me. Sometimes she was strict and critical, but her strictness and criticism were always wrapped in love.

No-one else in the world can criticize me like Griet. Her words reach down to my deepest inner being. She never fails to find the blind spot that I am unable (or don't want) to see. I have always taken her criticism to heart. In fact, I actively encourage it! I regard it as a gift from God that I have a sister who can call me to order whenever I go too far; who can point out that I might need to slow down, as long as I keep moving forward; who can teach me that I will never be able to care for others unless I first take care of myself.

At the same time, Griet is my best pupil, my first guinea pig and also a kind of try-out for this book! At all the key transition moments in her life, she took me into her confidence, using me as a soundboard for her own thoughts. While I am writing this, I am thinking: I often saw in her the potential and strength that she was unable to see in herself. Just as she is able to read me, so I am able to read her. If I see how she has given shape and form to her life, I am so proud of her and so grateful for her. She is not only a pillar of support for her children and her entrepreneurial husband, but radiates confidence and competence in all the functions she fulfils as a partner in PwC. There, in a highly result-oriented environment, she uses her connective and disarming talents to help her people, customers and partners reach their goals in harmony and understanding. She lets love rule.

The bonds of family create strong and deep roots. And the more roots a tree has, the stronger it is. That being said, there are also other roots that can help a tree grow. This book would not be complete without **Jeanne.** Jeanne, child-minder avant la lettre, was my second mother. Who cares that she never studied? She was full of worldly wisdom and love. For years she took care of me when my real mum couldn't be there. She surrounded me with love and pushed me forward. She was my petrol station, filling me with energy. There is no phase of my life that she didn't see from the front row. In her house she had a map of the world on which she pinned little flags for all the places I had worked in or visited. In that way, she stayed with me in her thoughts, long after the need for her to take care of me had passed. And what about me? For as long as she lived I never stopped asking my mother what I used to do daily when I was a child: 'Can I go to Jeanne's?' I do it still, but now only in my memories.

So that's it. That is the story I have been wanting to tell for so long. Now my circle is complete.

For you, my reader, I hope that you will set off on your own personal journey full of inspiration and confidence. That journey may be long or short, but driven on by the centrifugal force of your own dream-unfolding potential, sooner or later you will reach the end of your road – and then you will be able to fly like never before!

The global exists only through the generosity of the local.

KOEN VANMECHELEN

“**LET LOVE RULE** – that is the chicken in the community. Collaboration is necessary in her local biotope to give the chicken meaning at a global level. The love is found in the act of surrounding, and more particularly in its universal nature.’

an-Jacques Cassiman and Koen Vanmechelen, PHOTO ALEX DEYAERT

'In the first year of secondary school, Hilde told everyone who would listen that she had a life-size doll's house in her cellar at home. And not a day went by without her telling some story with her typical enthusiasm about the happenings in her home and her local village. Simple things became special: parents, having a brother or sister, making pancakes, going for a walk in the weekend, knitting or visiting the woman who did the sewing... Listening to her was easily as exciting as a Pippi Longstocking book! While life in my home slowly disintegrated bit by bit, a seed was nonetheless sown, from which a desire later grew to build a safe and secure haven in my own family. A strong example from a convincing ambassador helped me to achieve that dream.'

GEERTRUI OVERLOOP, ***a friend from secondary school***

ACKNOWLEDGEMENTS

This book is an example of Let Love Rule: we can achieve nothing in life alone. So a word of thanks to others is appropriate. How could it be otherwise? To start, I would like to go back to the earliest beginnings...

It is November 2016. For the third time, my sister Griet and I are attending the WOBI Congress in New York City. A month earlier I had broken my foot and almost saw my dream go up in smoke.

Later that same evening, Griet says to me in a tone of voice that makes clear she will not take 'no' for an answer: 'Hilde, we had planned to go to New York and we are going to New York, no matter what your foot is like. If I have to push you in a wheelchair, I will. But we're going. Understood?'

Day 1 of the conference. I am sitting next to Griet in my wheelchair. She says: 'Sis, when are you actually going to get around to writing that book of yours? When we're both old and gray?' It was during those days that the title *Dreamers who Do* first came into my head.

When I get home, I phone Barbara Simons, one of Griet's neighbours. She is just starting to make a name for herself as an independent writer as Elisa Candela. She is immediately willing to take part in my dream. Without her, this book would never have happened. She gets me. She can see into my head, my heart, my soul. And what she sees she magics into words with her pen, so that it becomes shareable. Her husband Wouter Keirse, a psychiatrist-psychotherapist, is her checkpoint for when 'deeper-lying theories' come into play.

On the same day that I phone Barbara, the seeds are sown for what will very quickly become our 'dream team'. Early on in the story Barbara brings in Annemie Mermans and her graphics bureau 'Meer wit'.

Annemie thinks along with us and translates everything into forms and images. When the door to LannooCampus opens, Niels Janssens also comes on board of our 'dream team' boat. Niels adds a chair for the reader in our thinking and together with his colleague Tim Moriën helps to spread the word. Miet Vanbergen, my organizational alter ego, also joins our project, to make sure – as she makes sure in so many other parts of my life – that everything is carried out with the necessary efficiency and discipline. In daily life, she is my right hand at TRAJECTUM. For years, we have been playing together – to use the words of Simon Sinek – 'the infinite game'.

It turns out that Koen Vanmechelen – this is how human networks operate – has been a friend of Barbara's for years. We sit around a table together and soon discover how different paths have led us to the same essence. Thank you, Koen, for opening your heart, for your generosity, for your giving and for involving your entire team.

Lenny Kravitz, at the time of writing these words I do not yet know you personally. It is not easy to explain just how much you have been my secure base, especially in recent years and in particular since I started TRAJECTUM. Be that as it may, your music has been the backbone in my four-step model: dream, stand, push and let love rule.

I would also like to express my gratitude to my friend Philippe Cognet, who for me so powerfully underlines what really matters, both in business and in life. Philippe, it was not without good reason that you were the first person with whom I shared my euphoria, when it became clear that a publisher was willing to embrace my long-cherished book dream.

Thanks also to Charles-Antoine Janssen, Willem de Jager, Isis Mulleman, Nadine Montens, Alain Maus and Annie Swennen, who made time and were willing to share with us what lives deep in their heads and hearts.

Charles-Antoine, I am grateful that you wanted to share your story in these pages, so that people from one world can catch a glimpse of another, and vice versa. What you have started with ToolBox is phenomenal: whether we have profit or non-profit background, our common aim is 'no separation'!

Willem, meetings in life make us what we are. What a privilege to have met you. You offer an answer to my desire as an engineer to unravel and demystify 'people'.

Isis, you came into the book via Barbara. What strength, what a wonderful example of how you can come to the core of your own being – and so move closer to others – through listening to your body.

Nadine, I am so pleased to have known you as a wise woman on whom I can so often rely.

Alain, you walked into my life as a young man. For me, you are a perfect example of how people can blossom and grow, if you give them space.

Annie, you also came into my life via Barbara. Thank you for your generosity. I am so grateful for this new meeting

Alexandre Mars, you too undoubtedly deserve a place in my gratitude. It's a pity that your busy agenda made a meeting during the writing process impossible. Even so, you remain a shining example of courage and perseverance.

My heartfelt thanks also go to a number of other people, who in their own words formulated for me what you can do to help push other people's dreams: Kees Broeren, Ignaas Declercq, Heidi De Roover, Roel Fransen, Geertrui Overloop, Olli-Matti Toivanen, Iris Vande Walle, Lies Van Rompaey and Didier Vercruysse. I am delighted to be your stove!

Geertrui, how wonderful of you to write down with such care for this book the things that I perhaps unconsciously knew. I am happy to give you that final word.

Dearest guides, although I do not (yet) know you personally, you are my secure bases. You have made it possible for me to push this dream – the writing of a book with a four-step model – into the world.

Simon Sinek, even before you became famous, I had latched on to your first TED talk. The power and simplicity of your model touched me deeply. For this reason, I am happy to do all I can to help further spread the message of your dream!

George Kohlrieser, I first saw your book lying around somewhere in my sister's house (she hadn't yet read it). I picked it up and was instantly charmed. I took it home and read it from cover to cover – more than once. When I met you in Rome during the 2012 WIN Conference, where you presented *Care To Dare,* I knew it immediately: this is something I can make use of, especially the result-based focus and the link between outcome and bonding.

Maya Angelou, it was via Oprah Winfrey that I learnt about your books and listened to your interviews. I was star-struck! I so want more people to get to know you and hope that this book can help in some small way to make that possible.

William Ury, I knew your early work, but it was with *Getting to Yes with Yourself* that you really hooked me. When I saw you in conversation with Simon Sinek, I knew that with you my circle was complete.

Thank you to all these guides for daring to stand up and go into the world, so that I had the good fortune to meet them.

Remembering the words of Koen Vanmechelen – 'The global exists only through the generosity of the local' – I would also like to thank Malorie Moneaux for the French translation, Ian Connerty for the English translation and proof readers Philippe Cognet, Magali De Rijck and Jan Naets.

In addition to all the people I have mentioned here, who in word or deed have made a direct contribution to the book, I would also like to make room for everyone I have met in my life so far. And I would like to do this with the words of Johnny Hallyday in *Ça ne finira jamais*:

Je n'suis que la somme
Des mains qui se tendent
Des cœurs qui attendent
Je suis ceux qui m'ont aimée

Je n'suis que la somme
Des mains qui se tendent
Des cœurs qui attendent
Je suis ceux que j'ai aimés...

And finally,

Where better can I end than with my family?

Mum, I am so happy that we have both lived for so long, and that we can now make time and have both the wisdom and the space to talk even more deeply about the things that matter in life. It's wonderful that your stories can now appear here in print as a source of inspiration for others.

Dad, your voice has not really been heard in this book. The damage to your brain took away your power of words. In recent years, your muteness has helped me understand a different dimension and our moments of silence together are now a source of intense pleasure to me. The countless times that you took to the stage during your career are burnt into my memory. You would first disappear for a couple of hours into your office, surrounded by your books, to prepare. That's when you planted in me a seed to one day do the same. During your lucid moments, I tell you about the book and I can sense your pride. Like me, you too always believed in the need for guides to show us the way, providing us with wisdom that we first need to understand before we can build further on it and make our own story. (This was written when my father was still alive. He died on 15 April 2018, just months before the publication of my book).

Geert, my great example of 'living your dream', thank you for sharing your story here. I am so happy that I was so often able to go along with you, notwithstanding the reservations of your environment. Keep realizing your dream! I am there for you.

Griet, my dream sister.

And Jeanne, you are still here – always.

We can do nothing alone.

LITERATURE

FOR MORE, SEE: TRAJECTUM.BE/ THEBOOK

CHAPTER 1 — DREAM,

SIMON SINEK / startwithwhy.com

1. SINEK, S. (2011). *Start with Why.* London: Penguin Books.
2. SINEK, S. (2014). *Leaders Eat Last.* London: Penguin Books.
3. SINEK, S. (2016). *Together is Better.* London: Penguin Books.
4. SINEK, S. (2017). *Find your Why.* London: Penguin Books.

CHAPTER 2 — STAND,

GEORGE KOHLRIESER / georgekohlrieser.com

1. KOHLRIESER, G. (2006). *Hostage at the Table. How Leaders Can Overcome Conflict, Influence Others, and Raise Performance.* New Jersey: John Wiley & Sons.
2. KOHLRIESER, G. (2012). *Care to Dare. Unleashing Astonishing Potential Through Secure Base Leadership.* New Jersey: John Wiley & Sons.

CHAPTER 3 — PUSH,

MAYA ANGELOU / see the category 'Maya Angelou' in Wikimedia Commons for media files

1. ANGELOU, M. (1984). *I Know Why The Caged Bird Sings.* New York: Little Brown.
2. ANGELOU, M. (2015). *The Complete Poetry.* New York: Random House.

CHAPTER 4 — LET LOVE RULE

WILLIAM URY / williamury.com

1. URY, W. (2012). *Getting to Yes: Negotiating Agreement Without Giving In.* New York: Random House. (original edition: 1981)
2. URY, W. (2015). *Getting to Yes with Yourself. And Other Worthy Opponents.* San Francisco: Harperone.

ABOUT THE AUTHOR

Fascinated from an early age by the way things function, **HILDE HELSEN** started her career as an engineer in material sciences. As one of the first female engineers to occupy various senior management positions in multinational companies – where she was able to realize dream after dream – she became increasingly intrigued by the way people function. The strong bonds she was familiar with from her own safe family nest searched for and found their way in an intuitive manner to the work floor. Coaching, transition and personal growth form an increasingly large part of Hilde's daily thinking and actions. She has developed a unique coaching approach, in which the individual and his/her personality are central.

Connecting people is Hilde's unique talent; inspiring people to rise above themselves is her mission. In 2012, she founded TRAJECTUM, an organization that guides individuals (people) and organizations (systems) through transitions. Today, she dreams – in an unadulterated 'practice what you preach' style – of one day taking the platform at the annual international WOBI (World of Business Ideas) Congress... Her motto: *Plus est en vous* ('There is more in you').

PHOTO JOKE EMMERECHTS